Top 25 locator
(continues on
back cover)
←

D0933463

# CityPack
# Dublin

**DR PETER HARBISON
AND MELANIE MORRIS**

If you have any comments
or suggestions for this guide
you can contact the editor at
*Citypack@theAA.com*

**AA Publishing**
Find out more about AA Publishing and the
wide range of services the AA provides by
visiting our website at *www.theAA.com*

# About This Book

## SYMBOLS

➕ Map reference to the accompanying fold-out map and Top 25 locator map

✉ Address

☎ Telephone number

🕐 Opening/closing times

🍴 Restaurant or café on premises or nearby

🚉 Nearest railway station

🚌 Nearest bus route

🚢 Nearest riverboat or ferry stop

♿ Facilities for visitors with disabilities

✋ Admission charges: Expensive (over €6), Moderate (€4–6), and Inexpensive (€3 or less)

↔ Other nearby places of interest

❓ Other practical information

▶ Indicates the page where you will find a fuller description

ℹ Tourist information

## ORGANIZATION

This guide is divided into six sections:

● Planning Ahead, Getting There
● Living Dublin—Dublin Now, Dublin Then, Time to Shop, Out and About, Walks, Dublin by Night
● Dublin's Top 25 Sights
● Dublin's Best—best of the rest
● Where To—detailed listings of restaurants, hotels, shops, and nightlife
● Travel Facts—practical information

In addition, easy-to-read side panels provide fascinating extra facts and snippets, highlights of places to visit and invaluable practical advice.

The colours of the tabs on the page corners match the colours of the triangles aligned with the chapter names on the contents page opposite.

## MAPS

**The fold-out map** in the wallet at the back of this book is a comprehensive street plan of Dublin. The first (or only) map reference given for each attraction refers to this map. **The Top 25 locator maps** on the inside front and back covers of the book itself are for quick reference. They show the Top 25 Sights, described on pages 26–50, which are clearly plotted by number (**1**–**25**, not by page number) across the city. The second map reference given for the Top 25 Sights refers to this map.

# Contents

# Planning Ahead

## WHEN TO GO

Most visitors come between March and October, when the weather is at its best and there is a wider choice of activities. The best lodging deals are available from November to February, but some attractions are closed.

Dublin is temperate year-round but rain is frequent.

**TIME**

Ireland is five hours ahead of New York, eight hours ahead of Los Angeles, and the same as London.

## AVERAGE DAILY TEMPERATURES

| JAN | FEB | MAR | APR | MAY | JUN | JUL | AUG | SEP | OCT | NOV | DEC |
|-----|-----|-----|-----|-----|-----|-----|-----|-----|-----|-----|-----|
| 46°F | 46°F | 50°F | 55°F | 59°F | 64°F | 68°F | 66°F | 63°F | 57°F | 50°F | 46°F |
| 8°C | 8°C | 10°C | 13°C | 15°C | 18°C | 20°C | 19°C | 17°C | 14°C | 10°C | 8°C |

**Spring** (March to May) is mild with mostly clear skies and a mix of sunshine and showers. April and May are the driest months.

**Summer** (June to August) is bright and warm but notoriously unpredictable. July is particularly showery. Heat-waves are rare.

**Autumn** (September to November) often has very heavy rain and is mostly overcast, although still quite mild. Even October can be summery.

**Winter** (December to February) is not usually severe and tends to be wet rather than snowy. Temperatures rarely fall below freezing.

## WHAT'S ON

**January** *Dublin International Theatre Symposium.*
**March** *Dublin Film Festival.*
*St. Patrick's Day Festival (15–18 Mar).*
*St. Patrick's Day* (17 Mar).
**April** *Dublin Opera Spring Season.*
**April–May** *Heineken Green Energy Festival.*
**June** *Music Festival* in Great Irish Houses; usually includes a number within easy reach of Dublin.
*Bloomsday* (12–16 Jun): the hero of James Joyce's novel *Ulysses* is celebrated in word, walks, and liquid refreshment (➤ 23).
**July** *International Summer School* at University College Dublin.
*Guinness Blues Festival.*
**August** *Kerrygold Dublin Horse Show* in the Royal Dublin Society grounds.
**September** *All Ireland Hurling and Gaelic Football Finals.*
*Dublin Jazz Week.*
**October** *Dublin Theatre Festival.*
*Dublin City Marathon.*
**December** *Dublin Antiques & Fine Arts Fair.*

*National Crafts Fair.*
*Christmas Carols* in St. Patrick's Cathedral (selected Sundays and special dates).
*Dublin Opera Winter Season.*

**Listings**
The daily newspapers, both morning and evening, provide good coverage of what's on in Dublin. Pick up a copy of *In Dublin*, printed every two weeks, and look for *The Event Guide*, free from clubs, cafés, and restaurants around the capital. Both list events.

## DUBLIN ONLINE

### www.irish-architecture.com
Archéire (architecture eireann) is a diverse selection of architecturally interesting sites with the emphasis ranging from history and preservation to current architectural developments.

### www.temple-bar.ie
The official site of Temple Bar Properties, a company established in 1991 to revitalize the area as a cultural quarter. The site offers an insight into Temple Bar today, what the area has to offer, events, and future developments.

### www.ireland.com
An influential website of one of Ireland's daily newspapers, the *Irish Times*. You can check out what's on in Dublin and reserve accommodation online.

### www.heritageireland.com
This website contains useful in-depth information about six National Cultural Institutions, historical sites, gardens, and inland waterways managed by Dúchas, the Heritage Service.

### www.eventguide.ie
A comprehensive guide that dispenses details about forthcoming events at venues across Dublin, from theatre and cinema to live music and comedy.

### www.ireland.travel.ie
The main Irish Tourist Board site carries a wealth of information on everything you need to know about the whole of Ireland. There are sections on history, culture, events, activities, accommodation, and gastronomy, as well as plenty of practical tips.

### www.visitdublin.ie
The local tourist board site unveils every aspect of the city via its efficient search engine. You'll find up-to-date lisitings of accommodation, restaurants, shopping, nightlife, events, and attractions.

## GOOD TRAVEL SITES

### www.fodors.com
A complete travel-planning site. You can research prices and weather; book air tickets, cars, and rooms; ask questions (and get answers) from fellow travellers; and find links to other sites.

### www.dublinbus.ie
Everything you could possibly need to know about the public bus service, including how to buy the best tickets for your needs. Also information about the DART system.

## CYBERCAFÉS

### Global Internet Café
Claims the fastest connection in Ireland.
➕ K7  ✉ 8 Lower O'Connell Street  ☎ 878 0295; www.globalcafe.ie
◉ Mon–Fri 8–11; Sat 9–11; Sun 10–11  🕹 From 75c per 15 minutes.

### Central Cybercafé
Small friendly café. Scanning and CD burning for no extra cost.
➕ k9  ✉ 6 Grafton Street  ☎ 677 8298
◉ Mon–Fri 8–11; Sat 9–11; Sun 10–10  🕹 From 75c per 15 minutes.

5

# Getting There

## ENTRY REQUIREMENTS

Visitors to Ireland must have a current passport (or official identity card for EU nationals), valid for the duration of their stay. UK citizens do not need a passport but should carry a driver's licence, birth certificate, or similar identification. The maximum stay permitted in Ireland for non-EU citizens is six months.

## MONEY

The euro is the official currency of Ireland. Bank notes in denominations of 5, 10, 20, 50, 100, 200, and 500 euros and coins in denominations of 1, 2, 5, 10, 20, and 50 cents, and 1 and 2 euros, were introduced on 1 January, 2002.

€50

€200

€500

## ARRIVING

Dublin Airport is 11km (7 mi) north of the city and has flights to Britain, mainland Europe, and North America, as well as to a few other cities in Ireland. Ferries from the UK sail into the ports of Dublin and Dun Laoghaire, 14.5km (9 mi) south of the city.

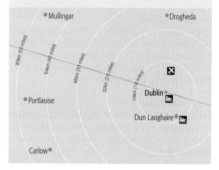

### ARRIVING BY AIR

For information on Dublin Airport ☎ 704 4222. *Airlink* runs between the airport and the main city bus station only. The journey takes around 20–30 minutes and costs €4.45. An alternative is Aircoach, costing €5, which makes several stops and runs every 15 minutes 5AM–11.30PM.

The taxi stand is outside the arrivals area. Taxis are always metered, and a journey to the city centre should cost around €15–19. Several car rental companies have desks in the arrivals area.

### ARRIVING BY BOAT

Ferries from Holyhead sail into the ports of Dublin and Dun Laoghaire throughout the year. The journey takes around 3 hours 15 minutes on a traditional ferry or 1 hour 45 minutes via the high speed options.

Taxis and buses operate from both ports into the city. The DART light train is easily accessible from Dun Laoghaire which is 12 km (7.5 mi) from the city centre). When travelling by car from Holyhead terminal, take the N31 to Blackrock. Turn left onto Mount Merrion Avenue and continue to the N11. Turn right and head north to get into town. From Dublin Port take Alexander Road west, turn left at the Point Depot and follow "city centre" signs.

### ARRIVING BY TRAIN
There are two main line stations in Dublin. Passengers from the north of Ireland arrive at Connolly Station, while trains from the south and west operate in and out of Heuston Station. Buses and taxis are available at both stations. Irish Rail is at ☎ 836 6222.

### ARRIVING BY CAR
Traffic drives on the left. Congestion in Dublin is increasing, and parking is expensive and limited. Avoid rush hours, keep out of bus lanes, and use designated parking areas. Traffic wardens take their job seriously, and penalties are severe. Most hotels and guest-houses have parking for guests. Always lock your car and keep belongings out of sight.

### GETTING AROUND
Buses are the usual way of getting around in Dublin but service can be unreliable. The bus number and destination (in English and Irish) are displayed on the front. *An Lar* means city centre. Buy tickets on the bus (exact change needed) or, before boarding from Dublin Bus office or some newsstands; timetables are also available here. Busáras, the main bus terminus, is north of the River Liffey on Amiens Street.
The DART is a light rail service running from Malahide in the north of the city to Greystones in the south. The main city-centre stations are Connolly (north side) and Pearse (south side). Trains run at least every 5 minutes at peak times, otherwise every 15 minutes Mon–Sat 6.30AM–11.30PM and less frequently Sun, 9.30AM–11PM. Buy tickets at the station.
Taxis are in short supply, especially at night. Taxi stands are found outside hotels, train and bus stations, and at locations such as St. Stephen's Green, Dame Street, O'Connell Street, and Dawson Street.
For more transport information ► 91–92.

For more transport information ► 91–92.

### INSURANCE
Check your insurance coverage and buy a supplementary policy if needed. EU nationals receive medical treatment with form E111. Obtain this form before travelling. Full health and travel insurance is still advised

### VISITORS WITH DISABILITIES
Access for wheelchair users has improved dramatically in Dublin over the years. Most public buildings and visitor attractions have ramps and lifts. However, it is wise to phone in advance. Dublin Bus are now incorporating features into their buses to make them more user-friendly for customers with disabilities.

The National Rehabilitation Board (☎ 668 4181) publishes two useful booklets: *Guide for Disabled Persons* and *Accommodation Guide for Disabled Persons*. The Disability Federation of Ireland can provide a list of helpful organizations in Dublin (✉ 2 Sandyford Office Park, Dublin 18 ☎ 295 9344).

# Living
# **Dublin**

# Dublin Now

Above: *a café area in the Powerscourt Townhouse Centre in Dublin*
Above right: *Georgian architecture in Dublin*

The Celtic Tiger, as the Irish economy was nicknamed in the 1990s, has seen an unprecedented boom over the last decade, kick-started when Dublin became European City of Culture in 1991. The mood is buoyant, positive, forward-looking, and vital. The culture is cosmopolitan, youthful, and buzzing. The pubs, clubs, and museums now rival those of many other European cities. The redeveloped district of Temple Bar, the further development of the Old City and Docklands area, and new ventures north of the River Liffey at Smithfield show that Dublin is no backwater. No wonder thousands travel to Dublin from all over Europe for weekend breaks.

## TEMPLE BAR AND THE OLD CITY

• Business flourished in Temple Bar beginning in the early 17th century but the area fell into decline in the early 20th century and by the late 1980s had been proposed as the site for a new bus terminal. Objections were vociferous and the city's "left bank" began to take off. Today, pedestrian-friendly and with restricted vehicle access, this is a vibrant cultural quarter and the main draw for tourists with its mix of restaurants, shops, pubs, and bars. Gentrification is spreading as the Old City development is launched around Cow's Lane, Dublin's oldest district.

### THE H.A.R.P. PLAN

• The Historic Area Rejuvenation Project is 110 ha (270 acres) north of the Liffey where lack of investment has led to a decline in the condition of the neighbourhood. The project is a framework for the regeneration of the area, both economically and socially.

Above left: *Trinity College, Dublin*
Above: *the reading room in the National Library*

With the economic boom came an influx of artists, musicians, film-makers, chefs, and designers attracted by tax concessions and cheap property—and by 2001 the *Irish Times* declared Ireland the most expensive place in Europe to buy a house.

How do Dubliners perceive their city? Many Dubs, as they are known, prospered on the strength of the new service and IT industries. They have bought homes in smart leafy suburbs and commute to work, drink in trendy wine bars, eat in the stylish restaurants, and live the life of the new Dublin. Others maintain that the renovated Temple Bar is too "gentrified" and that the development so loved by visitors and many young Dubliners has ruined the place.

### THE *CRAIC*

• *Craic* (pronounced "crack") is a word that describes fun, laughter, and an overall good time. In Ireland people, places, and events can all be "great craic." Pubs are a great place for the *craic*, not just for drinking; they are where people join together for music, singing, and talking.

Above: *the Chimney at Smithfield Village*
Above right: *The Millennium Bridge over the River Liffey*

And what about the traffic that clogs the city each morning and evening, and what about the traditional way of life?

Fortunately Dublin has managed to retain a great deal of its intimacy and its traditional Irish music and dance thrive; it is still possible to fall upon an impromptu music session. The old city is still there, especially beyond Grafton Street and trendy Temple Bar. Away from these beaten paths shops still specialize in communion clothes for boys and girls, who still dress up for their big day, and you can stroll in the squares and parks, visit old pubs, wander by a canal, and discover real Dubliners going about their daily lives. On the north side of the River Liffey in Moore Street sturdy women still sell fruit, vegetables, pop posters, and chocolate from prams, evoking modern-day images of Molly Malone, the oyster-selling heroine of Dublin's anthem. The population still cheers heartily for winning Gaelic football and hurling teams.

The schemes to develop the more run-down parts of the city are not just for tourists. The large area north of the Liffey reaching to Collins

## THE CHIMNEY

• Dublin's only observation platform, at Smithfield Village, offers a 360-degree panorama of the city. Built in 1895 as a distillery chimney 75m (220ft) high, it now has a two-tiered glass platform, accessible via a panoramic glass lift. You can have a champagne breakfast at the top or watch the sun set over Phoenix Park.

Barracks in the west and O'Connell Street in the east will incorporate residential development as well as shops, offices, hotels, and cultural venues. The DART (Dublin Light Railway Transit) has recently been extended farther north and south of the city. The new Luas (meaning "speed") light rail system, due to open in 2003, will give access from the suburbs into the heart of the city. This is all part of a larger public transport network for Dublin which may ease the traffic problems.

Above: *Temple Bar Film Centre*

## LITERARY GIANTS

• Starting with Jonathan Swift's *Gulliver's Travels* in 1726 the Irish literary tradition continues with Bram Stoker's *Dracula* in 1897 and the works of Oscar Wilde, George Bernard Shaw, and W. B. Yeats in the late-19th century through to Dublin's most famous literary giant James Joyce in the early 20th century and his successors Sean O'Casey, Samuel Beckett, Brendan Behan, and Patrick Kavanagh. Throughout the city you'll find literary references in the form of museums, statues, and memorabilia. Current literati include Edna O'Brien, Roddy Doyle, and Maeve Binchy.

Above: *Irish dancers*
Right: *the bar and pub scene is buzzing*
Far right: *the colourful St. Patrick's Day Parade*

## FASHIONABLE DISTRICT

• Dignitaries and celebrities often stay 10 minutes from the centre, on the southeast side of Dublin city. The fashionable area of Ballsbridge and Lansdowne Road is near the international rugby ground, the Royal Dublin Society's showgrounds, and the exclusive embassy belt with its excellent restaurants and classy hotels.

The pub scene is booming. The number of clubs and modern bars has increased. And although some old-style pubs have suffered, those that have moved with the times and serve food and provide traditional Irish music are flourishing. Meanwhile, café culture is booming: With even the slightest hint of sunshine, patrons fill tables set up outside. Food lovers celebrate the city's restaurants, where tastes range from Thai, Japanese, and Indian to Russian, Mexican, and Italian while traditional Irish food is not forgotten either.

## HA'PENNY BRIDGE

• This attractive cast-iron footbridge spanning the Liffey and leading to Temple Bar dates from 1816 and takes its name from the toll demanded until 1919—a halfpenny. One of Dublin's best-known landmarks, it has been repainted in an historically correct off-white.

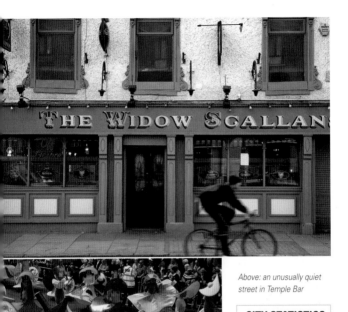

*Above: an unusually quiet street in Temple Bar*

Theatre, film, music, and comedy venues provide a huge range of contemporary and established entertainment while the museums are second to none, many of them in the Georgian district, renowned for its architecture.

Mountains, green fields, and the coastline mark the city limits, and the wide-open space of Phoenix Park, the pretty squares, and the broad River Liffey breathe life into the centre. If the city's pace becomes too much, you have only to head out a few stops on the DART to the attractive coastal resorts for a round of golf or a walk by the shore (not to mention the opportunity to visit excellent seafood restaurants).

## CITY STATISTICS

• Car ownership in Dublin increased tenfold between 1996 and 1998.

• The number of tourists has increased from 2.5 million in 1997 to 6.4 million in 2000.

• In 1672 Dublin had 1,180 ale-houses and 93 breweries. By 1999 this had dropped to 850 pubs and only one major brewer.

• Approximately 43 percent of Ireland's population is under 25.

15

# Dublin Then

Above: *Jonathan Swift*
Right: *soup kitchen at the
start of the Great Famine*
Far right: *Easter Rising 1916*

## BEFORE AD 1000

The Celts landed in Ireland in the 4th century BC and their influence remains even today. Their religious rites included complex burial services. Archaeological excavations have produced some magnificent gold pieces and jewellery, some of which can be seen in Dublin's National Museum (► 46).

According to legend St. Patrick converted many of Dublin's inhabitants to Christianity in the 5th century AD. In 841 Vikings established a trading station, probably near present-day Kilmainham. The Vikings moved downstream, to the area around Dublin Castle, in the 10th century.

**1014** High King Brian Boru defeats the Dublin Vikings.

**1172** After Norman barons invade Ireland from Wales, King Henry II gives Dublin to the men of Bristol.

**1348–51** The Black Death claims one third of Dublin's inhabitants.

**1592** Queen Elizabeth I grants a charter ▪for the founding of Trinity College.

**1700s** Dublin's population expands from 40,000 to 172,000.

**1712** Work starts on Trinity College Library.

**1713** Jonathan Swift is appointed Dean of St. Patrick's Cathedral.

**1714** Start of the Georgian era, Dublin's great period of classical architecture.

**1742** Handel conducts his *Messiah* in the city's old Musicke Hall.

**1745** The building of Leinster House (now home of the Irish Parliament) leads to new housing south of the river.

**1759** The Guinness Brewery is founded.

**1760–1800** Dublin reaches the height of its prosperity.

| 1782 | Irish Parliament secures legislative independence from Britain. |
| --- | --- |

*President Kennedy in Dublin*

| 1800 | The Act of Union is passed and the Irish Parliament abolishes itself, prefacing a period of urban decline. |
| --- | --- |
| 1847 | Soup kitchens are set up around Dublin during the Great Famine. |
| 1916 | The Easter Rising. |
| 1919 | First session of *Dáil Éireann* (the Irish Parliament) in Mansion House. |
| 1922 | Civil War is declared. After 718 years in residence, British forces evacuate Dublin Castle. |
| 1963 | Visit by President John F. Kennedy. |
| 1979 | The Pope says mass in Phoenix Park to more than 1.3 million people. |
| 1991 | The inauguration of Ireland's first female president, Mary Robinson. |
| 1998 | The Good Friday Agreement finally sees a lasting cease-fire in Northern Ireland. |
| 2001 | IRA decommissioned in December. |
| 2002 | The euro becomes the official currency of Ireland. |

## EASTER RISING

With the founding of the Gaelic League in 1893 and the Abbey Theatre in 1904, the movement for independence gathered momentum in Ireland. Frustrated republicans capitalized on England's preoccupation with World War I to stage a rising in 1916 and declare an independent Republic in Dublin's General Post Office. It was doomed to failure but the execution of several of the insurrection's leaders made rebels out of many Irish royalists, leading five years later to the creation of an Irish Free State. The Anglo-Irish Treaty was signed in 1921, followed by a Civil War in 1922, lasting 22 months. In 1936 the Free State became known as Eire under a new Constitution. The Republic finally became a reality in 1949.

# Time to Shop

Below: *Dublin has a long literary heritage and plenty of bookshops*

The delight of shopping in bustling Dublin lies in the compact nature of the city and the proximity of the best shopping areas to one another.

## KNOW YOUR *BODHRÁN* FROM YOUR BANJO

The *bodhrán* (pronounced "bough-rawn") is a simple and very old type of frame drum made of wood with animal skin—usually goat—stretched over the frame and beautifully decorated. It is played with a double-ended stick unlike most others, which are struck with the hands. Played for centuries in Ireland it came on to the world stage in the 1960s with the rise of the Irish band The Chieftains. If you can't master the technique, try hanging it on your wall!

Major fashion houses are represented as are traditional, second-hand, and retro shops.

Generally, the best department stores and a wider variety of shops are north of the river on O'Connell Street and Henry Street, a busy pedestrian area where Irish and international chain stores, sports retailers, discount outlets, musicians, and street vendors jostle for attention. Pedestrianized Grafton Street, south of the river, is smarter. On either side are shops and department stores along with flower sellers, street musicians, hair braiders and jewellery stalls, and a fine selection of the international and Irish fashion designer shops that underpin Dublin's new cosmopolitan atmosphere.

Sample bohemian South Great Georges Street, filled with second-hand clothes and ethnic stores. Busy Temple Bar's cobbled, winding streets are full of unique shops and craft design outlets. Dublin's antiques quarter, Francis Street, has beautiful furniture, Irish silver, and wonderful one-of-a-kind pieces.

*Middle: St. Stephen's Green Centre has three floors of shops*

Ireland is renowned for its handmade crafts. Look for Aran knitwear—every sweater is unique. A Donegal tweed cap or hat makes a good souvenir. Jewellery has a special place in Dublin; look for the exquisite replicas of the Tara Brooch, Claddagh rings, and Celtic knots mixing modern design with tradition. Waterford Crystal has moved with the times and now uses designer John Rocha to produce clean, minimalist styles. Belleek is famous for its distinctive baskets—and don't forget the delicate Irish linen and lace.

In home interior shops you'll find modern designs based on traditional patterns—visit Cow's Lane near Temple Bar. Dublin is the place to buy traditional musical instruments. And although much is mass produced in the Far East, Celtic kitsch is still part of Irish culture. Leprechauns, shamrocks, and shillelaghs are in profusion.

### LOCAL DELICACIES

Breads, farmhouse cheeses, and salmon are a few of the local delights, along with handmade fresh cream chocolates and truffles. Bewley's cafés sell their exclusive teas and coffees in attractive containers. Look for Guinness-flavoured toffees and Irish Porter cake. The Old Jameson Distillery sells all manner of Irish whiskey flavoured items—truffles, jams, fudge, chutney—but don't forget a bottle of the real thing.

19

# Out and About

## GUIDED CITY TOURS

**By Bus**
**Dublin Bus** ☎ 873 4222
**Guide Friday** ☎ 676 5377
**Irish City Tours** ☎ 458 0054
**Old Dublin Tours** ☎ 670 8822 or 605 7705
**On Foot**
**Dublin Footsteps** Tours start from Bewley's Café, Grafton Street ☎ 496 0641 🅾 Literary and Georgian Dublin Jun–Oct: Mon, Wed, Fri, Sat 10.30AM
**The Walk Macabre** Visit scenes of murder and intrigue. Start at the Main Gates, St. Stephen's Green (opp Planet Hollywood).
☎ Bookings: 087 677 1512
🅾 Nightly 7.30
**Historical Walking Tours** Two hours around the Trinity College area. Start at the college's front gate.
☎ 845 0241 🅾 May–Oct: daily 11, 12, 3; Nov–Apr: Fri, Sat, Sun noon

## INFORMATION

**MALAHIDE CASTLE**
**Distance** 13km (8 miles)
**Journey Time** 45 minutes
☎ 846 2184
🅾 Apr–Oct: Mon–Sat 10–5; Sun, public hols 11–6. Nov–Mar: Mon–Sat 10–5; Sun, public hols 11–5
🚌 42
🚆 From Connolly Station to Malahide, then a 10-minute walk

## ORGANIZED SIGHTSEEING

City tours by bus leave from O'Connell Street. Buy tickets on board or at Dublin Tourism in Suffolk Street. There are also many guided walks to choose from (▶ panel). The Jameson Literary Pub Crawl visits pubs frequented by literary

giants, with readings from the works of Beckett, Yeats, Joyce, and Behan. The tour lasts two hours fifteen minutes, starting from the Duke pub, Duke Street (☎ 670 5602 🅾 Nov–Easter: Thu, Fri, Sat 7.30PM, Sun noon, 7.30. Easter–Oct: nightly 7.30, Sun noon, 7.30). The Musical Pub Crawl takes you to Dublin's most popular musical hostelries, finishing with a lively musical *seisiún*. It starts from the Oliver St. John Gogarty pub, Fleet Street (☎ 478 0193 🅾 Mid-May–late Oct: nightly 7.30, Feb–mid-May: Fri, Sat 7.30PM).

## EXCURSIONS
### MALAHIDE CASTLE

Malahide Castle stands in a wooded area, north of Dublin. Apart from an interlude during the rule of Oliver Cromwell, the castle stayed in the hands of the Talbot family from c1200 until 1976. The core of the castle is a medieval tower and in the adjoining banqueting hall, the walls are hung with portraits. Most furnishings are Georgian. A separate building houses the beautifully detailed rolling stock of the Fry Model Railway. Outside are opportunities for walking and the Talbot Botanic Gardens (May to September).

## POWERSCOURT

Careful restoration has converted the 18th-century Palladian mansion into an excellent gallery of shops with a terrace restaurant. It is in a dramatic setting, with the cone-shaped Sugar Loaf mountain in the distance. To the south, the

house looks out over magnificently proportioned stepped terraces, with ornamental sculpture, and a statue throwing a jet of water high in the air. Gardens stretch to either side; the one to the east is Japanese, the other walled with wrought-iron Bavarian gates. (The story goes that when the terraces' designer, Daniel Robertson, went to inspect the work every morning, he was pushed around in a wheelbarrow, swigging sherry.) You can walk to the waterfall 5km (3 miles) away, but it is easier to get there by car.

## GLENDALOUGH

Glendalough ("valley of two lakes") was one of Ireland's most venerated monasteries. Situated at the end of a long valley stretching deep into the Wicklow hills, it grew up around the tomb of its founder, St. Kevin, who died in 618. The core of the old monastery consists of a roofless cathedral (c900), a well-preserved Round Tower, and St. Kevin's Church, roofed with stone. Overlooking the Upper Lake, about a mile away, is another enchanting church called Reefert. There are good walks in the surrounding woods.

### INFORMATION

**POWERSCOURT**
**Distance** 19km (12 miles)
**Journey Time** 1 hour
☎ 204 6000
🕐 9.30–5.30 (gardens close at dusk)
🚌 48 to Enniskerry village, then 20-minute walk
🚆 DART to Bray, then feeder bus to Enniskerry
❓ Waterfall inadvisable on foot

Far left: Malahide Castle
Left: *just north of Enniskerry lies the spectacular 3,400 acre Powerscourt Estate; the beautiful gardens include Japanese and Italian sections and a waterfall*

### INFORMATION

**GLENDALOUGH**
**Distance** 48km (30 miles)
**Journey Time** 1 hour 15 minutes
☎ 404 45325
🕐 Interpretative centre 9.30–5, later in summer
🚌 Can be reached on coach tours from Dublin. The most direct route if driving is the N11 (M11) south

# Walks

## INFORMATION

**Distance** 1.5km (1 mile)
**Time** 45 minutes
**Start point**
★ George's Quay
➕ L8
🚇 Tara Street
**End point** Merchant's Quay
➕ J9
🚇 None nearby

## ALONG THE QUAYS WITH GANDON

The English-born architect James Gandon (1743–1823) played an important role in the beautification of Dublin during the late 18th century. This walk begins and ends with his two finest creations. Follow the footpath along the Liffey to see Gandon's impressive buildings reflected in the water.

Start at George's Quay and look across to the Custom House, a magnificent neoclassical building, built by Gandon between 1781 and 1791. At O'Connell Bridge, glance left along Westmoreland Street to see the portico (c1784–89) that Gandon added to the Old Parliament House, now the Bank of Ireland (► 40). Continue upstream past the metal bridge, known as the Ha'penny Bridge (1816). At Capel Street Bridge, look south along Parliament Street to Thomas Cooley's City Hall, built in 1769, some time before Gandon arrived in Dublin. Turn to admire the seahorses on Grattan Bridge, and Betty Maguire's Viking Boat sculpture (20th century). Continue past the City Offices on your left, where excavations unearthed a Viking site in the 1970s, until you reach Merchant's Quay. Here you have the best view of Gandon's second masterpiece, the Four Courts, built between 1786 and 1802 (► 54).

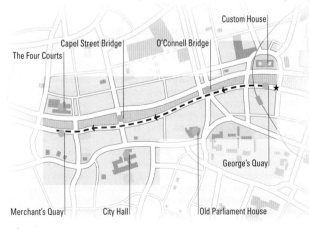

## A Short Joycean Odyssey

In *Ulysses*, James Joyce had his fictional hero, Leopold Bloom, traverse many parts of Dublin during a single day, 16 June 1904. On the same day every year, costumed Joyceans retrace their hero's footsteps. To capture the Bloomsday spirit, follow a section of the route, indicated by 14 bronze plaques set into the pavement.

Start in Middle Abbey Street at Eason's shop (Nos. 79–80) then continue around the corner to Champion Sports (49 O'Connell Street) and on to the northwest corner of O'Connell Bridge, where Bloom experienced "a puffball of smoke" from a barge. Crossing to the south side of the Liffey, Bloom passed the Ballast Office (corner of Aston Quay and Westmoreland Street). "The mockturtle vapour and steam of newbaked jampuffs rolypoly" poured from Harrison's Restaurant—still on the east side of Westmoreland Street. Soon you come to a statue of poet Thomas Moore, on a traffic island north of Trinity College. Walk to the bottom of Grafton Street where Bloom priced field glasses in Messrs. Yeats and Sons (now ICS Building Society) and continue up Grafton Street. Turn left onto Duke Street and left again for Molesworth Street; a pub once stood at Nos. 10–11. The final plaque is outside the National Museum.

### INFORMATION

**Distance** 1km (0.6 miles)
**Time** 45 minutes
**Start point**
★ Middle Abbey Street
🚌 K7
🚆 Tara Street
**End point** Kildare Street
🚌 L9
🚆 Pearse

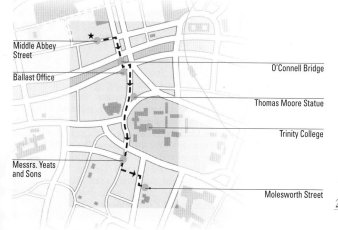

Middle Abbey Street

Ballast Office

O'Connell Bridge

Thomas Moore Statue

Trinity College

Messrs. Yeats and Sons

Molesworth Street

# Dublin by Night

Above: *The Custom House*
Right: *The Oliver St. John Gogarty pub in Temple Bar*

## MERRION SQUARE & BAGGOT STREET

Evening light is kind to Dublin's Georgian architecture. Under illumination the imposing buildings and elegant square resemble the set of a magnificent period drama.

Starting at the Davenport Hotel on Lower Merrion Street stroll along the north side of Merrion Square. Follow the east side of the square then turn left into Upper Mount Street, before walking around St. Stephen's Church. A left turn onto Herbert Street brings you to Baggot Street. Turn right and walk towards town. Where Baggot Street becomes Merrion Row, turn right down Merrion Street to admire the National Gallery and government buildings.

Whether you like clubs, trendy cocktail bars, or traditional pubs, there is no shortage of venues. Dublin's theatres are famous—playwrights such as Brian Friel continue to garner accolades in London and New York—and feature a wide repertoire of plays and opera for the more cultural evening, or perhaps you prefer to catch one of the latest releases at the cinema.

### ANYONE FOR A DRINK?

Dublin pubs are an institution and pub crawls make for a great night out, especially when you try to track down the thickest and tastiest pint of Guinness or Murphy's, or a lighter lager—Harp is brewed in Dublin. Although most pubs close at 11PM, 11.30PM, or 12.30AM, some pubs, bars, and clubs have a late licence—until 2.30 on one or more nights. Watch out for local leaflets announcing Irish music or jazz and rock sessions in many pubs and bars.

### LAUGHTER OR DANCING?

Expanding fast, Dublin's comedy scene sees lots of new talent emerging and comedy clubs seem to open all the time. There is stand-up comedy at many pubs every night; on open-mic nights comedians and other acts battle it out to be acclaimed as the night's best act. The Comedy Cellar on Wicklow Street still features international comedians such as Ardal O'Hanlon and Tommy Tiernan. Dance clubs, which have multiplied dramatically since the mid-1990s, pulse with hardcore, garage, techno, and chart toppers.

# DUBLIN's
## top 25 sights

The sights are shown on the maps on the inside front cover and inside back cover, numbered **1**–**25** across the city

# Kilmainham Gaol

*No escape—chained serpents over the entrance*

## HIGHLIGHTS

- East wing
- 1916 corridor with cells
- Museum display

## INFORMATION

- 🔡 B9; locator map off A3
- ✉ Inchicore Road, Kilmainham
- ☎ 453 5984
- 🕐 Apr–Sep: daily 9.30–6 (last admission 4.45). Oct–Mar: Mon–Sat 9.30–5.30 (last admission 4); Sun 10–6 (last admission 4.45)
- 🍴 Café
- 🚆 Heuston
- 🚌 51B, 68, 69, 78A, 206
- ♿ Call in advance for wheelchair assistance
- 💶 Moderate
- ↔ Irish Museum of Modern Art (► 27), Collins Barracks (► 28)
- ❓ Guided tours only—pre-book to avoid queues

**Leading figures in every rebellion against British rule since 1798 are associated with Kilmainham Gaol and, for many Irish people, their imprisonment or death represents freedom achieved through sacrifice.**

**Prisoners** A deserted gaol may seem an unusual place to spend a few hours, but with its stark and severe interiors, Kilmainham has a fascination which is more inspirational than morbid. Opened in 1796, and altered frequently since, the gaol is made up of tall interlinked blocks in the centre, flanked by exercise and work yards. During the course of its long history, it held both civil and political prisoners, the earliest of whom were participants in the 1798 rebellion. The flow continued throughout the following century and included the "Young Ireland" rebels of 1848 (Europe's "Year of Revolution"), the Fenian suspects of 1867, and notable parliamentarians in the 1880s.

**Conditions** Overcrowding created appalling conditions when the Great Famine of 1845–49 drove many to petty crime. Closed in 1910, the gaol was reopened during the 1916 rebellion in Dublin to receive insurgents whose execution in the prison in the May and June of that year turned the tide of public opinion in many parts of Ireland in favour of the armed struggle. During the Civil War of the early 1920s, the gaol again housed anti-government rebels including many women, and four Republican leaders were executed. The doors were closed in 1924, and the abandoned gaol was eventually restored by volunteer groups between 1960 and 1984. It is now cared for by the State, which has installed an excellent museum display and other facilities.

# Irish Museum of Modern Art

**The Royal Hospital at Kilmainham, once a haven for retired soldiers, is now an ultramodern cultural centre where regularly changing exhibitions showcase the latest trends in contemporary art.**

**Shelter** The most important surviving 17th-century building in Ireland, the Royal Hospital at Kilmainham was founded as the Irish equivalent of the Invalides in Paris and the Chelsea pensioners' hospital in London. The architect, surveyor-general Sir William Robinson, laid the structure around an open quadrangle, and created a covered arcade around three sides of the ground floor where residents could stroll outdoors even in poor weather. Work was completed by 1686, except for the tower and steeple, which were added by Sir Thomas Burgh (➤ 28) between 1701 and 1704.

**Transformation** A hospital until 1922, the building was transformed 70 years later into the National Centre for Culture and the Arts, covering music and art. The Irish Museum of Modern Art is Ireland's leading national institution for the collection and presentation of modern and contemporary art. The museum's mission is to foster within society an awareness, understanding, and involvement in the visual arts presenting a wide variety of artists' work in a programme of exhibitions. It possesses its own collections, such as the excellent Madden-Arnholz collection of historic prints (from Dürer onwards) and the New York Portfolio, Gordon Lambert's gift of prints by prominent American artists. Selections are frequently on display on the ground and upper floors, and the museum regularly stages changing exhibitions of modern art from Europe and beyond.

*Royal Hospital steeple*

## HIGHLIGHTS

- Covered arcade
- Tympana
- Permanent collections
- Visiting exhibitions

## INFORMATION

- ✚ C9; locator map off A3
- ✉ Royal Hospital, Military Road, Kilmainham
- ☎ 612 9900
- 🕐 Tue–Sat 10–5.30; Sun and public hols noon–5.30
- 🍴 Café
- 🚆 Heuston
- 🚌 51B, 68, 69, 78A, 206
- ♿ Good except for East Wing
- 💶 Free
- ❓ Free guided tours of exhibitions Wed and Fri 2.30PM; Sun 12.15

27

# Collins Barracks

**Here you can view the decorative arts and social history collections of the National Museum—products of Irish artists and craftspeople that have been hidden from view for many years.**

- Old barracks building
- Fonthill vase
- Multi-storey clock
- "The Way We Wore" exhibition

## INFORMATION

- ✚ E7; locator map off A2
- ✉ Benburb Street
- ☎ 677 7444
- 🕐 Tue–Sat 10–5; Sun 2–5
- 🍴 Café 🚉 Heuston
- 🚌 25, 25A, 66, 67, 79, 90
- ♿ Very good, difficult in parts
- 💷 Free
- ❓ Book inexpensive tours in advance

*Floral tapestry exhibit*

**The building** Sir Thomas Burgh (1670–1730), best known as architect of the Old Library in Trinity College (▶ 44), also designed Dublin's large Royal Barracks, just over a mile outside the city. Built in 1704, on high ground overlooking the River Liffey, they were handed over in 1922 to the Irish State, which named them after Michael Collins, the revolutionary leader killed in an ambush towards the end of the Civil War. Until decommissioning in 1997, they were generally thought to be the oldest military barracks still in use anywhere in the world.

**Exhibits** The barracks opened as an annexe to the National Museum in the same year, greatly strengthening Dublin's cultural and historical focus. The items on display range from the 17th century to the present day and comprise Irish silver, glass, and furniture, all of which reached a high point of artistic excellence, particularly in the 18th century. Don't miss the Chinese porcelain Fonthill vase, which has managed to survive its well-documented wanderings in Asia and Europe, or the clock whose winding chains extend the height of two floors. Opened for the new millennium is the permanent exhibition of 250 years of Irish clothing and jewellery, "The Way We Wore," where the Irish echoed the styles of the fashion conscious of Europe.

## Guinness Storehouse

**Think Dublin, think Guinness. An integral part of the city's economy and history, the "black stuff" is known throughout the world. The Guinness Experience should not be missed.**

**What's in a glass?** As you enter the 1904 building through a stone arch an escalator takes you up into the centre of the building. You then walk into what is described as a large pint glass. Within this glass structure your journey through the production process of a pint of Guinness begins. Simple, dramatic displays show the four basic ingredients, hops, barley, yeast, and water, all of which you can touch, feel, and smell. The displays provoke the senses as indicated on the huge wall label reading "Smells are delectable too, the heavy sleepy scent of hops—steam hot metal, sweat."

**Mine's a pint** You follow the pint as it makes its way through the brewery of the past founded by Arthur Guinness in 1759—a past still much in evidence today. Old machinery is cleverly utilized, doubling up as interactives to give you more information. From the brewing process you go to the transportation section, with large scale models showing how Guinness has reached the far-flung corners of the world. The advertising display is great fun, with popular memorabilia and a hall of fame recalling classic Guinness advertisements. Finally, you learn how Guinness has affected many aspects of Irish life as supporter of the arts, festivals, and sport. You finish your journey at the top of the glass, in the bar, with a splendid view over Dublin and it's here you get your free pint.

### HIGHLIGHTS

- Glass pint structure
- Brewing exhibition
- Transport section
- Round tower
- Classic advertisements and memorabilia
- Rooftop view

### INFORMATION

- F9; locator map off A3
- St. James's Gate
- 404 4800
- Daily 9.30–5
- Brewery Bar, Gravity Bar
- 51B, 78A from Aston Quay; 123 from O'Connell Street
- Excellent
- Expensive
- Shop

*A fine view over Dublin*

# Glasnevin

## INFORMATION

**Botanic Gardens**
➕ H1; locator map off B1
✉ Glasnevin Hill Road
☎ 837 4388 or 837 7596
🕐 Summer: Mon–Sat 9–6; Sun 11–6. Winter: Mon–Sat 10–4.30; Sun 11–4 (glasshouses/ alpines are restricted)
🚇 Drumcondra
🚌 13A, 19, 134
♿ Good except for some greenhouses
🎫 Free
❓ Guided tours available by prior arrangement

**Cemetery**
➕ G1
✉ Finglas Road, Glasnevin
☎ 830 1133
🕐 Daily 9–5
🚇 Drumcondra
🚌 40, 40A, 40B, 40C
♿ Good, except to crypt
🎫 Free

Top: *Great Palm House of 1884 in the National Botanic Gardens*

**Once the site of a monastery, this leafy suburb has two well-wooded neighbours separated only by a tall stone wall—the National Botanic Gardens and the National Cemetery.**

**Botanic Gardens** Ireland's most extensive and varied collection of plants are carefully tended here. Generously laid out over 19.5 ha (47 acres), the gardens were founded in 1795. The curvilinear greenhouses, built by Richard Turner, a Dubliner who created a similar structure for Kew Gardens in London, are among the finest surviving examples of 19th-century glass-and-iron construction. Many of the plants housed within originate from Southeast Asia; one rarity, the handkerchief tree (so called because the whitish leaves enclosing each flower resemble handkerchiefs), comes from China. The rose bush near the entrance was propagated from one in County Kilkenny that inspired Thomas Moore's celebrated poem *The Last Rose of Summer*. An education and visitor centre opened in 2000 gives a good insight into the Botanical Gardens.

**Cemetery** The adjoining cemetery is reached by a separate entrance just over a mile away. Its graves are a *Who's Who* of modern Ireland's formative years: Charles Stewart Parnell, Michael Collins, and Eamon de Valera. At the foot of Ireland's tallest Round Tower lie the remains of Daniel O'Connell (1775–1847), who founded the cemetery and liberated Irish Catholics from repressive religious legislation. Kavanagh's pub, outside the old entrance, is known locally as the Grave-diggers'; thirsty grave-diggers would pass their shovels through an opening in its wall and a pint of beer was added to restore their spirits.

# Dvblinia

**If you want to know just what made Dublin's medieval ancestors tick, check out the Dvblinia exhibition, a scale model of the medieval city with tableaux and an audio-visual show.**

**Vivid re-creation** Dvblinia, as the town was first recorded on a map *c*1540, is a colourful re-creation of medieval Dublin life housed in the Victorian-era former Synod Hall. After the Vikings had re-established the city in this area during the 10th century, Hiberno-Norsemen and Normans occupied it from 1170 until the end of the Middle Ages—the time-span covered by Dvblinia.

**Excavations** One of the most impressive features is the scale model that shows Dublin as it was around 1500; Christ Church Cathedral is inside the city walls and St. Patrick's Cathedral beyond. Thirty years of excavations in the Dvblinia area have uncovered many fascinating artefacts such as leatherwork, pottery decorated with amusing faces, floor tiles, jewellery, and ships' timbers, which are also on view in the exhibition. An audio-visual presentation of the city's history complements the series of life-size model tableaux that illustrate episodes from the past. Climb the 96 steps inside the tower of 15th-century St. Michael's Church, incorporated into the Synod Hall when it was built, for great views of the city and the River Liffey. Dvblinia was voted Best Smaller Museum in the Museum of the Year Award, 2001.

## HIGHLIGHTS

- Re-creation of medieval Dublin
- Scale model
- Interactive re-created Medieval Fair
- Medieval artefacts
- View over Dublin

## INFORMATION

- ✛ H9; locator map B3
- ✉ St. Michael's Hill, Christchurch
- ☎ 679 4611
- ◷ Apr–Sep: daily 10–5. Oct–Mar: Mon–Sat 11–4
- 🚌 51B, 78A, 121, 123
- 🍴 Café
- ♿ Dvblinia: good. Tower and bridge: none
- 💰 Moderate
- ↔ Christ Church (► 32)
- ❓ Pre-bookable tours

Top & below: *medieval Dublin life re-created*

# Christ Church Cathedral

**Christ Church Cathedral, the public heart of the city in the Middle Ages, is not only Dublin's oldest stone building but also perhaps the Normans' outstanding contribution to Irish architecture. It reflects 1,000 years of history and worship in Ireland.**

**History** The older of Dublin's two cathedrals, Christ Church was founded by the Norse king Sigtryggr Silkenbeard in 1038. The northern side of the choir and the south transept are the oldest parts of the existing stone structure and have been dated back to just before 1180, indicating that the Normans started the building shortly after they took over the city, using masons brought over from the west of England. The early Gothic nave, dated c1226–36, also reflects English influence. Its vault collapsed in 1562, leaving the north wall with a remarkable outward lean of about 51cm (20 inches).

**Restoration** The whole building would now be a romantic ivied ruin but for the intervention of the Dublin whiskey distiller Henry Roe, who paid for its reconstruction between 1872 and 1878. The work was carried out under the direction of the great English Victorian architect George Edmund Street, who added flying buttresses to keep the whole edifice standing. Look for the effigy of a knight in armour near the entrance, traditionally thought to represent the great Norman knight, Strongbow (Robert de Clare). In the Peace Chapel of Saint Laud is the heart-reliquary of the cathedral's co-founder, Saint Laurence O'Toole, who died in Normandy in 1180. An unusual feature is the original crypt, extending the entire length of the cathedral and housing the "Treasures of Christ Church" exhibition with a video of the cathedral's history.

*Top: 14th-century knight's effigy in the nave*

## HIGHLIGHTS

- 12th-century south transept
- Leaning north wall
- Knight's effigy
- Crypt and "Treasures of Christ Church"

## INFORMATION

- ✠ H9; locator map B3
- ✉ Christchurch Place
- ☎ 677 8099
- 🕐 Mon–Fri 9.45–5; Sat, Sun 10–5. Treasures: Mon–Fri 9.45–5; Sat 10–4.45; Sun 12.30–3.15
- 🚌 51B, 78A, 121, 123
- ♿ None
- 💷 Requested donation €3; Treasures exhibition: moderate

# St. Patrick's Cathedral

**"Here is laid the body of Jonathan Swift, Doctor of Divinity, Dean of this Cathedral Church, where fierce indignation can no longer rend the heart. Go traveller, and imitate, if you can, this earnest and dedicated champion of liberty."**

*Top: monument of Archbishop Thomas Jones (c1620).*
*Above: the nave*

**Literary connections** Jonathan Swift's epitaph is a fitting tribute to the personality most often associated with St. Patrick's Cathedral. The author of *Gulliver's Travels*—written as a political satire but enjoyed by generations of children—Swift was the cathedral's fearless and outspoken Dean from 1713 until his death in 1745. He and his beloved Stella, rumoured to have been his wife, are buried inside the modern entrance.

**History** Founded as a church in 1192, and raised to cathedral status in 1219, St. Patrick's was built in the early English Gothic style and completed by 1284. The fact that Dublin has two Protestant cathedrals is something of a paradox in a predominantly Catholic city and country. Like Christ Church (► 32), St. Patrick's was heavily restored in the 19th century, entirely with funds from the wealthy Guinness family.

**Flags** The monuments in the cathedral and on its walls include the tomb and effigy of the 17th-century adventurer Richard Boyle, Earl of Cork, and a memorial to the great Irish bard and harpist Turlough Carolan (1670–1738). In the south choir aisle are two of Ireland's rare 16th-century monumental brasses. The flags in the north transept were carried by Irish regiments, who experienced both victory and tragedy in battle; those in the choir commemorate the noble order of the Knights of St. Patrick. The cathedral organ is the largest in Ireland.

## HIGHLIGHTS

- Swift's bust and epitaph
- Medieval brasses
- Memorial to Carolan
- Organ
- Living Stones Exhibition

## INFORMATION

- ✚ H10; locator map B4
- ✉ St. Patrick's Close
- ☎ 453 9472
- 🕐 Mon–Fri 9–6; Sat Mar–Oct 9–6, Nov–Feb 9–5; Sun Mar–Oct 9–11, 12.45–3, 4.15–6, Nov–Feb 10–11, 12.45–3
- 🚌 50, 54A, 56A
- 🚻 None 🅿 Moderate
- ↔ Marsh's Library (► 34), Christ Church (► 32)

# Marsh's Library

- Old-world atmosphere
- Oak bookcases
- "Cages" for rare works
- Books and manuscripts

## INFORMATION

- H10; locator map B4
- St. Patrick's Close
- 454 3511
- Mon, Wed, Thu, Fri
  10–12.45, 2–5; Sat
  10.30–12.45
- 50, 51A, 56A
- None
- Moderate
- Dvblinia (► 31), St.
  Patrick's (► 33), Christ
  Church (► 32)

*Alcoves lined with
leather-bound tomes*

**This magnificent example of an 18th-century scholar's library has changed little since it opened nearly 300 years ago. One of the few buildings here to retain its original purpose, it remains a calm oasis of scholarly learning.**

**Rare legacy** In 1701, Archbishop Narcissus Marsh (1638–1713) built Ireland's first public library close to St. Patrick's Cathedral and filled it with his own books and 10,000 others purchased in 1705 from the Bishop of Worcester. Two years later, it was given official legal standing when the Irish parliament passed an Act for "settling and preserving a public library." The building is one of the city's rare legacies from the reign of Queen Anne and was designed by Sir William Robinson, responsible for the Royal Hospital at Kilmainham (► 27), using distinctive grey Dublin limestone on one side and red brick on the front.

**Precious books** Inside, the long gallery is flanked on each side by dark oak bookcases adorned with carved and lettered gables topped by carvings of an archbishop's mitre. At the end of the L-shaped gallery are three alcoves or "cages," where readers were locked with the library's precious books. As an extra safeguard, chains were attached to the books (though not to the readers). The volumes reflect the founder's wide-ranging interests, and the oldest example is Cicero's *Letters to his Friends*, published in Milan in 1472. The library also possesses some 300 manuscripts, displayed with other items in glass-fronted cases.

# Chester Beatty Library & Gallery

**Sir Alfred Chester Beatty is one of the few people to have been made an honorary citizen of Ireland. For bequeathing to the nation in 1956 such rare and priceless art collections, he richly deserved this award.**

**Hidden treasure** The library and oriental art gallery named after its founder and benefactor, Sir Alfred Chester Beatty (1875–1968), is one of Dublin's jewels yet one that many visitors unwittingly ignore. The collection is housed in a converted Georgian building.

**Masterpieces** Alfred Chester Beatty, a successful mining engineer born in New York and knighted for his services to Britain as an advisor to Winston Churchill during World War II, devoted an important part of his life to the search for manuscripts and *objets d'art* of the highest quality. The collections range from *c*2700 BC up to the 19th century, and stretch geographically from Japan in the east to Europe in the west. Religious writings range from one of the earliest known New Testament papyri to the Korans, all masterpieces of calligraphy. There is a wealth of Persian and Mughal miniature paintings as well as wonders of the East such as Burmese and Siamese painted fairy-tale books or *parabaiks*, Chinese silk paintings and jade snuff bottles, and Japanese *netsuke* and woodblock prints. Exhibitions are focused on two diverse themes—Great Religions of the World and Secular Arts and Patronage. The library won the Gulbenkian Heritage Council Irish Museum of the Year Award in 2000.

Top: *Chinese ceiling in the old Library*
Right: *Oriental art exhibit*

## HIGHLIGHTS

- New Testament papyri
- Koran manuscripts
- Persian and Mughal paintings
- Jade snuff bottles

## INFORMATION

- ✚ H9; locator map C3
- ✉ The Clock Tower Building, Dublin Castle
- ☎ 407 0750
- ⊙ Mon–Fri 10–5 (closed Mon Oct–Apr); Sat 11–5; Sun 1–5
- 🍴 Café
- 🚉 Tara Street
- 🚌 49A, 50, 51B, 54A, 56A, 77A, 121, 123, 150, 206
- ♿ Good
- 🎟 Free (charge for special events)
- ❓ Audio-visual. Free guided tours

# Dublin Castle

## HIGHLIGHTS

- Powder Tower
- State Apartments
- Chapel Room

## INFORMATION

- ✚ J9; locator map C3
- ✉ Dame Street
- ☎ 677 7129
- 🕐 Mon–Fri 10–5; Sat, Sun, and public hols 2–5. State Apartments closed occasionally for functions
- 🍴 Restaurant
- 🚆 Tara Street
- 🚌 49A, 50, 51B, 54A, 56A, 77A, 121, 123, 150, 206
- ♿ State Apartments: good Powder Tower: none
- 🎧 Varies
- ↔ Christ Church (➤ 32)
- ❓ Gardens, open Mon–Fri, do not form part of tour

*The Throne Room in the State Apartments*

**How many buildings in Europe can claim to have been the centre of a country's secular power for longer than Dublin Castle, the headquarters of English rule in Ireland for more than 700 years?**

**Ancient site** Dublin Castle, now used for State occasions, presidential inaugurations, and occasional European summit meetings, stands on the site of a much older Viking settlement. It occupies the southeastern corner of the Norman walled town, overlooking the long-vanished black pool or *dubh linn* that gave the city its ancient Irish name. The castle's defined rectangular shape was determined from the start in 1204 with the construction of a twin-towered entrance on the north side and stout circular bastions at each corner. The excavated remains of one of these, the Powder Tower, shown on the guided tour, rested on an earlier Viking foundation and was attached to the city wall beside an arch, beneath which water flowed from the old castle moat.

**Interior** After a fire in 1684, the interior was almost entirely rebuilt in the 18th and early 19th centuries. On the south side of Upper Castle Yard are the State Apartments, where the English king's viceroy lived until the castle was handed over to the Irish State in 1922. These regal rooms form the second half of the guided tour, which starts in the Powder Tower.

# Hugh Lane Gallery

**Degas, Monet, Corot, and Renoir are among the Impressionist artists whose paintings are on display in this wonderful gallery that also looks back over a hundred years of the Irish arts, including paintings and stained glass.**

**Philanthropist** The Hugh Lane Gallery of Modern Art fills a niche between the old masters on display in the National Gallery (➤ 48) and the ultramodern creations in the Irish Museum of Modern Art at Kilmainham (➤ 27). Built between 1761 and 1763 by the Earl of Charlemont to the designs of Sir William Chambers (➤ 50), the gallery now bears the name of Sir Hugh Lane who was drowned when the *Lusitania* sank in 1915. Before his death, Sir Hugh added a codicil to his will stating that a group of 39 of his Impressionist pictures that were in London, including works by Corot, Degas, Manet, Monet, and Renoir, should go to Dublin. However, the codicil was unwitnessed with the result that London claimed the canvases and kept them until it was agreed that each city should display half of them at any time in rotation. You can visit the reconstructed studio of Francis Bacon, complete with its entire contents of more than 7,500 items.

**Modern art** Irish artists of the last hundred years, including Osborne, Yeats, Orpen, Henry, and Le Brocquy, are well represented, and modern European artists include Beuys and Albers. Make sure you see the stunning examples of stained glass by Clarke, Home, and Scanlon.

## HIGHLIGHTS

- Impressionist paintings
- Jack Yeats, *There is no night*
- Orpen, *Homage to Manet*
- Works by Roderic O'Connor
- Stained glass
- Francis Bacon's studio

## INFORMATION

- ✚ J6; locator map C1
- ✉ Charlemont House Parnell Square North
- ☎ 874 1903
- 🕐 Tue–Thu 9.30–6; Fri, Sat 9.30–5; Sun 11–5
- 🍴 Café
- 🚆 Connolly
- 🚌 3, 10, 11, 13A, 16A, 19A
- ♿ Few 🎟 Free
- ❓ Call for individual tours

*Augustus John's 1920 portrait of Miss Iris Tree*

# Dublin Writers Museum

## HIGHLIGHTS

- Letters of Thomas Moore and Maria Edgeworth
- Yeats manuscript
- Indenture signed by Swift

## INFORMATION

- J6; locator map C1
- 18 Parnell Square North
- 872 2077
- Mon–Sat 10–5; Sun and public hols 11–5. Late opening Jun–Aug: Mon–Fri 10–6
- Café
- Connolly Station
- 10, 11, 11A, 11B, 13, 13A, 16A, 19A
- None
- Moderate
- Recorded audio guide. A combined ticket is available with James Joyce Museum and the Shaw Birthplace

**For centuries a meeting point for gifted writers, Dublin has become the centre of a great literary tradition. This museum celebrates their diverse talents and displays a truly fascinating range of memorabilia.**

**Great Irish writers** Many languages have been spoken by Ireland's inhabitants down the centuries, including Norse, Irish, and Norman French, but it was with the establishment of English as the *lingua franca* in the 17th century that Dublin's literary reputation was established. Restoration dramatists such as George Farquhar were followed 50 years later by the brilliance and acerbic wit of Jonathan Swift. At the end of the 19th century, a new era dawned with the emergence of Oscar Wilde, whose epigrams enthralled the world. Around the turn of the 20th century, William Butler Yeats, encouraged by the flourishing Irish literary movement, helped found the Abbey Theatre, which opened in 1904. His contemporary, George Bernard Shaw, and subsequent Irish writers such as James Joyce, Samuel Beckett, and Brendan Behan have continued to open new horizons in world literature.

**Displays** Photographs, paintings, and other items linked with Ireland's literary titans are backed up with lots of explanatory material. First editions and rare volumes abound, and there are original letters of the poet Thomas Moore and the 19th-century novelist Maria Edgeworth, a manuscript of W. B. Yeats and an indenture signed by Jonathan Swift. As well as bronze busts of George Bernard Shaw and Oscar Wilde, the museum has portraits of celebrated and lesser-known artists. Take time to look at the house itself—the stucco work is one example of the craftsmanship used in the 18th-century homes of Dublin's wealthy.

*Top: the first-floor portrait gallery of many famous authors who have graced the Dublin scene*

# General Post Office

**The General Post Office symbolizes the birthplace of modern Ireland. Overlooking one of Europe's widest thoroughfares, it was the city's last great public building created in the neoclassical style.**

**Classical splendour** The imposing breadth of O'Connell Street, north of the River Liffey, was the brainchild of the Wide Street Commissioners in the second half of the 18th century—a prescient decision given the volume of today's traffic. The street's focal point was Nelson's Pillar, surmounted by the victor of Trafalgar. At a height of 14m (135ft), it was the city's best vantage point until it was toppled by a bomb in 1966. The only remnants of the street's classical splendour are the walls of the General Post Office, designed by Francis Johnston (1814–18). The Ionic portico extends over the footpath at the front, and John Smith's statues of *Hibernia* (with spear and harp), *Mercury* (with a purse), and *Fidelity* dominate the skyline.

**Easter Rising** Inside the north entrance is a plaque with beautifully cut letters recording the reading of the Proclamation of the Irish Republic in the building during the Easter Rising of 1916 (▶ 17). The insurgents were forced to surrender after the interior was reduced to rubble (the bullet chips on the portico columns are a sobering reminder of the bitter struggle) and 16 were later executed. However, their stand led to the creation of modern Ireland and a salute is given here in their memory at Dublin's annual St. Patrick's Day parade.

*Oliver Sheppard's statue of the* Dying Cuchulainn *(1911–1912) commemorates the 1916 Rising*

## HIGHLIGHTS

- Ionic portico decoration
- Statues above portico
- Plaques inside entrances

## INFORMATION

- ✚ K7; locator map D2
- ✉ O'Connell Street
- ☎ 705 7000
- ◷ Mon–Sat 8AM–8PM; Sun and public hols 10–6.30
- 🚊 Tara Street
- 🚌 Cross-city buses
- ♿ Few
- 💶 Free
- ❓ None

# Bank of Ireland

**This great semicircular building was the focus of Ireland's glorious years of freedom at the end of the 18th century, when the city reached the zenith of its architectural and artistic achievement.**

*Edward Smyth's statue of Liberty over Gandon's east portico (1785–1789)*

## HIGHLIGHTS

- Exterior detail
- Former House of Lords
- Jan van Beaver tapestries
- Chandelier
- Bank of Ireland Arts Centre

## INFORMATION

- K8; locator map D3
- 2 College Green
- 677 6801
- House of Lords: Mon–Fri 10–4; Thu 10–5. Bank of Ireland Arts Centre, Foster Place entrance: Tue–Fri 10–4
- Tara Street
- Cross-city buses
- Few  Free
- Tours of House of Lords Tue 10.30, 11.30, 1.45

**Harmony** The Bank of Ireland, overlooking College Green, began life as the upper and lower houses of the old Irish Parliament, which gained its legislative independence in 1782 but saw its members bribed to vote itself out of existence 18 years later. Its first architect was the young Edward Lovett Pearce, who designed the recessed south-facing "piazza" of Ionic columns (*c*1729–39) and the rooms behind it, of which the old House of Lords is still intact and frequently made accessible to the public. In it hangs a wonderful Dublin crystal chandelier (1788) of 1,233 pieces, and two fine tapestries (1733) by Jan van Beaver—one of King James II at the 1689 Siege of Londonderry, the other of King William of Orange astride his steed at the 1690 Battle of the Boyne. The fireplace in the north wall of the room is the work of a Dublin carver, Thomas Oldham. You can visit the Bank of Ireland Arts Centre in the old bank armoury for the "Story of Banking" exhibition.

**Alterations** The architect James Gandon (➤ 22) added the curving and windowless screen and the east-facing Corinthian portico between 1785 and 1789, and a corresponding portico was added to the west side some years later. After the parliament was dissolved, the building was sold in 1802 to the Bank of Ireland, on condition that it be modified to prevent it from being used again for public debate. These changes were carried out by Francis Johnston, whose work forms the basis of the contemporary banking rooms.

# University Church

**This Byzantine-style church has to be one of Dublin's most unusual ecclesiastical edifices; the only building where Cardinal John Henry Newman left a record of his presence.**

**Vision** Convert, champion of intellectual freedom, and one of the world's first ecumenists, Newman (1801–90) spent the years 1854 to 1858 in Dublin. While he was in the process of setting up what he hoped would be the "Catholic University of the English tongue for the whole world" (➤ 42), he acquired the garden plot between Nos. 86 and 87 St. Stephen's Green and set about building a church to promote his ideals. Jutting out onto the sidewalk is the porch, which through a later addition, has carved capitals of early Christian design that suggest the Byzantine splendour within.

**Byzantine interior** In the nave, the richly coloured Irish marble slabs panelling the side walls are particularly striking, and frame a niche containing a bust of Newman by Thomas Farrell. Look for the attractive little birds on the capitals of the columns dividing the marble panels. John Hungerford Pollen, an architect and friend of Newman, came over from England to supervise the building. Pollen also painted the ceiling and executed the wonderful golden apse decorated with a tree of life with various echoes of medieval Flemish figures and the architecture of an ancient Roman basilica. After its completion in 1856, Newman described the church as "the most beautiful one in the three Kingdoms."

## HIGHLIGHTS

- Marble panelling
- Carved birds on capitals
- Ceiling
- Golden apse

## INFORMATION

- 🔳 K10; locator map D4
- ✉ 87A St. Stephen's Green
- 🕐 Mon–Sat 9–5.30; Sun 10–1, 5–6
- 🚌 Cross-city buses
- 🚆 Pearse
- ♿ None
- 💷 Free
- ↔ Newman House (➤ 42)

*Byzantine splendour*

# Newman House

## HIGHLIGHTS

- Apollo room
- Upper floor Saloon
- Staircase
- Gerard Manley Hopkins' room

Apollo *in stucco by the Lafranchini brothers*

## INFORMATION

- ✚ K10; locator map D4
- ✉ 85–86 St. Stephen's Green
- ☎ 716 7422
- ◉ Jun–Sep: Tue–Fri 12–5 (by appointment rest of year)
- 🍴 Café
- 🚆 Pearse
- 🚌 Cross-city buses
- ♿ None
- 💰 Moderate
- ❓ Guided tours only

**The exuberant stucco work of this house on St. Stephen's Green provided the baroque and rococo background to nurture the literary genius of John Henry Newman, Gerard Manley Hopkins, and James Joyce.**

**Ornamentation** Named after one of the 19th-century's greatest liberal intellectuals, Newman House is actually two great houses. No. 85 was built in 1738 for Captain Hugh Montgomery, a member of Parliament wealthy enough to employ Switzerland's great Lafranchini brothers to decorate the walls and ceilings with stucco ornament. Their most notable achievements are the figures of Apollo and the nine muses on the ground floor, and the extravagant ceiling of the Saloon, which stretches the entire length of the upper floor.

**Experiment** In 1754, another parliamentarian, Richard Chapel Whaley, bought No. 85 and just over 10 years later, built the house at No. 86. The interior here is embellished with equally exuberant stucco work, particularly the stair-case. Whaley's religious intolerance contrasted sharply with the ethos of Cardinal Newman, who used the mansion in the 1850s for his great experiment in bringing education to the Catholic masses—a liberal Victorian university. Called the Catholic University of Ireland, it was intended as a rival to the long-established Protestant Trinity College. On the top floor is the room once occupied by Gerard Manley Hopkins, a Jesuit priest and fellow-countryman; one of the founders of modern poetry, he was professor of classics at the college from 1884 to 1889. Later alumni included James Joyce, who studied here between 1899 and 1902.

# James Joyce Centre

**Of all the literati to grace the Dublin scene during the 20th century, James Joyce has undoubtedly earned the greatest reputation internationally, so it is fitting that a whole house is devoted to the writer and his work.**

**Connections** This 18th-century house, in an impressive street of equally well-restored Georgian redbrick residences just 275m (300 yards) from O'Connell Street, is home to the James Joyce Centre. Initially, its Joycean connection was established through a dancing master called Denis J. Maginni, who leased one of the rooms in the house around the turn of the 20th century and appears as a character in *Ulysses*. A more immediate connection is the presence of members of the novelist's family, including his nephew Ken Monaghan, who show visitors around the house and give them the opportunity to listen to tapes of Uncle James reading from *Ulysses* and *Finnegan's Wake*.

**Memorabilia** Take time out to browse in the extensive library and gaze at the portraits of those featured in the master's work, either under their own name or a pseudonym. You can also see the original doorway rescued from the now-demolished No. 7 Eccles Street, the imagined residence of the Ulyssean hero, Leopold Bloom, as you head for the small café at the back of the house. The centre is also a starting point for an hour-long walking tour (payable separately) of Joycean sites on the north side of the city.

## HIGHLIGHTS

- Joyce family members
- Recordings
- Library
- Portraits of characters in *Ulysses*
- No. 7 Eccles Street door

*Jacques Emile Blanche's portrait of James Joyce*

## INFORMATION

- ✚ K6; locator map D1
- ✉ 35 North Great Georges Street
- ☎ 878 8547
- 🕐 Mon–Sat 9.30–5; Sun 12.30–5
- 🍴 Café open in summer
- 🚉 Connolly
- 🚌 3, 10, 11, 13, 16, 19
- ♿ Few  🅿 Moderate
- ❓ Guided tours of house and Joycean Dublin

43

# Trinity College

## HIGHLIGHTS

- Book of Kells
- Book of Durrow
- Book of Armagh

## INFORMATION

- ✚ K8; locator map D3
- ✉ College Green
- ☎ 608 2308
- ⏰ Old Library: Oct–May: Mon–Sat 9.30–5; Sun 12–4.30. Jun–Sep: Mon–Sat 9.30–5; Sun 9.30–4.30
- 🍴 Café on campus
- 🚆 Pearse
- 🚌 Cross-city buses
- ♿ Good
- 💷 Moderate
- ❓ College tours May–Sep

*A page from the Book of Kells (c800)*

**Stroll around the grounds of the famous college and visit the library where you will find one of the most joyously decorative manuscripts of the first Christian millennium, the Book of Kells.**

**Surroundings** An oasis of fresh air, Trinity College is also the noblest assemblage of classical buildings in the city. Inside, the open square marked with Arnoldo Pomodoro's sculpture *Sphere within Sphere* (1982–83) is surrounded on three sides by some of Dublin's finest modern and ancient buildings—Paul Koralek's New Library (1978) to the south, Benjamin Woodward's splendidly carved Museum building (1853–55) to the east, and Thomas Burgh's dignified Old Library (1712–32) to the west. In 1857, Woodward altered Burgh's building and made its barrel-vaulted upper floor into one of Ireland's most breathtaking spaces—lined with books from floor to ceiling and decorated with marble busts.

**Book of Kells** The library is an appropriate setting for Ireland's greatest collection of medieval manuscripts. Among these, pride of place goes to the Book of Kells (*c*800), a Gospel book that has been bound in four separate sections so that its brilliantly ornamented pages and text may be viewed side by side. Displayed alongside are the important books of Durrow (*c*700) and Armagh (*c*800), the latter giving us most of the information we have about Ireland's patron saint, Patrick. The exhibition in the Old Library's main chamber gives useful background information about the collections.

# Heraldic Museum

**Every year, thousands of people come to Ireland in search of their roots, but even those without a drop of Irish blood will find this museum fascinating, both in its contents and context.**

**Heraldry** The Heraldic Museum, an integral part of the National Library, is housed in Dublin's most colourful mid-19th-century building—the former Kildare Street Club (1858–61), designed by Benjamin Woodward. (The decorative birds and amusing monkeys playing billiards and musical instruments among the window carvings are enough to make a visit worthwhile.) The museum occupies the club's former dining-room, beneath the tall ceiling off which hang modern banners of Ireland's ancient chieftain families. Needless to say, heraldry is everywhere—on the livery buttons of gentlemen's servants, on the crest of the Joyce clan of Galway, or on items of 19th-century Belleek pottery decorated with the coats of arms of Irish towns. Look for the colours of the Irish infantry regiments who fought in France during the 18th century as well as the mantle and insignia of the knightly Order of St. Patrick.

**Napoleon** Despite the emphasis on Irish family history, there are also objects from outside Ireland. You will find the arms of the city of Cologne, along with those of the Spencer-Churchill family (late 18th-century), Napoleon Bonaparte, and Sir Francis Drake. The 14th-century crusader badge made of pewter is another intriguing item. If you are inspired to trace your own Irish ancestry, enquire at the Consultancy Service of the National Library, a few doors along.

## HIGHLIGHTS

- Animal sculptures on facade
- Irish Chieftains Banners
- Colours of Irish infantry in France
- Arms of Napoleon
- Heraldic Insignia Exhibition

## INFORMATION

- L9; locator map E3
- ✉ 2–3 Kildare Street
- ☎ 603 0311
- ⏲ Mon–Wed 10–7; Thu, Fri 10–4.45; Sat 10–12
- Pearse
- Cross-city buses
- None
- Free
- National Museum (► 46)

Top: *decorative facade*

# National Museum

## HIGHLIGHTS

- Prehistoric gold
- Tara Brooch
- Ardagh Chalice
- Cross of Cong
- Viking exhibition
- Egyptian room

## INFORMATION

- ✚ L9; locator map E4
- ✉ Kildare Street
- ☎ 677 7444
- 🕐 Tue–Sat 10–5; Sun 2–5
- 🍴 Café
- 🚇 Pearse
- 🚌 Cross-city buses
- ♿ Ground floor good
- 🎫 Free
- ↔ Heraldic Museum
  (➤ 45), Natural History
  Museum (➤ 47),
  National Gallery (➤ 48)

*The 8th-century Ardagh Chalice in the Treasury Room*

**Most of Ireland's greatest treasures are housed in the National Museum. A visit here is a must for a deeper understanding of the country's history and culture since prehistoric times.**

Extensive collections For over a century, the twin institutions of the National Museum (1890) and the National Library have faced each other across the square leading to the *Dáil*, or Houses of Parliament. On the ground floor, the museum displays western Europe's most extensive collection of prehistoric gold ornaments, mostly dating from the Bronze Age (*c*1500–500 BC). These strikingly shaped pieces of glittering personal adornment were made from thin sheet or massive gold. Even more significant are the brooches, chalices, crosses, and croziers (AD 600–1200), largely the products of Ireland's early Christian monasteries, on show in the Treasury Rooms. Among the greatest gems in this dazzling collection are the 8th-century Tara Brooch, Ardagh Chalice, and the Derrynaflan Hoard. Also of interest is the "bog" burial. The body was discovered in 1821 in perfect condition and was dated to 440–200BC. Exposure has now caused severe detoriation.

Tribute Another room on the ground floor is concerned with the Easter Rising of 1916. Not to be missed upstairs are the contrasting exhibitions on pharaonic Egypt, Viking Dublin, and the 2001 Medieval Ireland display spanning the years 1150 to 1550.

# Natural History Museum

**The old glass cases and creaking floor-boards have changed little since the museum's inauguration in 1857, when Dr. David Livingstone gave the first lecture on his "African discoveries."**

**Fauna** The Natural History Museum is one of the four great national institutions flanking the Irish Houses of Parliament. The nucleus of its collection was assembled by the Royal Dublin Society long before it opened, and it has benefited greatly from subsequent gifts. Facing you as you enter is the skeleton of the giant Irish deer, better known as the Irish elk, with its impressive antlers. Beyond, is a great array of Irish furred and feathered animals as well as marine species ranging from the greater spotted dogfish and the exotic sunfish to giant lobsters.

**Dodo** The upper floor is given over to animals of the world, among them the great Irish wolfhound and a massive 20m (66-ft) long whale suspended from the ceiling. There is also a skeleton of the flightless dodo and a cluster of hummingbirds. Geology is something of a sideline but is represented by a meteorite that landed in 1810 on County Tipperary in central Ireland and took some two hours to cool down. A different kind of curiosity is the outfit worn by Surgeon-Major Thomas Heazle Parke (1858–93), of the Royal Army Medical Corps, who became the first Irishman to cross Africa from coast to coast. The explorer Sir Henry Morton Stanley contributed generously to Parke's statue in front of the museum.

## HIGHLIGHTS

- Giant Irish elk
- Great Irish wolfhound
- Fin whale
- Dodo skeleton
- Hummingbird
- Small meteorite

## INFORMATION

- ✚ L10; locator map E4
- ✉ Merrion Street
- ☎ 677 7444
- 🕐 Tue–Sat 10–5; Sun 2–5
- 🚉 Pearse
- 🚌 Cross-city buses
- ♿ Ground floor access only
- 💲 Free
- ↔ National Gallery (➤ 48), Number Twenty Nine (➤ 49)
- ❓ Optional inexpensive tours

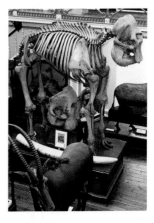

Top & right: *skeletons of the past on display*

47

# National Gallery

## INFORMATION

- ✚ L9; locator map E4
- ✉ Merrion Square West
- ☎ 661 5133
- 🕐 Mon–Sat 10–5.30; Thu 10–8.30; Sun 2–5
- 🍴 Restaurant, café
- 🅿 Pearse
- 🚌 Cross-city buses
- ♿ Very good
- 💰 Voluntary
- ↔ Natural History Museum (► 47), Number Twenty Nine (► 49)
- 📷 Public tours Sat 3PM; Sun 2.15, 3, and 4PM. Telephone for lectures

**Ireland's National Gallery enjoys considerable standing on the international scene as the home of one of Europe's premier collections of old masters.**

**Origins** Facing onto Merrion Square the National Gallery is set in relaxing green surroundings. The gallery was established in 1854 and opened in 1864 to display old master paintings as an inspiration to budding Irish artists of the mid-Victorian period. Its contents have expanded twenty-fold in the century-and-a-half since then, helped by numerous bequests. These include works by Vermeer, Velázquez, and Murillo; the legacy of one-third of George Bernard Shaw's residual estate enabled the Gallery to acquire important works by Fragonard and J. L. David, among others.

**Masterpieces** The Irish paintings, on the ground floor, show a progression from the 18th century onwards while the old masters, for which the Gallery is famous are on the next floor. Wide coverage is given to most European schools of painting—including icons, early Italians (Uccello and Fra Angelico), Renaissance (Titian, Tintoretto), Dutch and Flemish (G. David, Rembrandt, Rubens), early German (Cranach), Spanish (Goya), French (Poussin), and British (Reynolds and Raeburn, among others). The display also covers Impressionists and modern painters up to Picasso. A special room is devoted to watercolours and drawings—including 31 by Turner shown every January. The Millennium Wing, designed by Benson & Forsyth, and opened in 2002, houses a centre for the study of Irish art, temporary exhibition galleries, and an archive dedicated to the life and works of Ireland's most distinguished painter of modern times, Jack B. Yeats.

# Number Twenty Nine

**So many of Dublin's 18th-century houses are used as offices that it is a pleasure to see this rare example furnished in elegant period style.**

**The setting** Merrion Square epitomizes the graciousness of Georgian Dublin. Three of its four sides are surrounded by four-floor redbrick houses, each elegant doorway crowned by a handsome fanlight. The view from the south side towards St. Stephen's (also known as the Pepper Canister because of the shape of its cupola) is one of the city's most attractive streetscapes, and on the southeast corner of the square stands Number Twenty Nine, the only structure in Dublin to preserve the graceful middle-class domesticity of the 18th century.

**Nostalgia** You enter, as servants did, through the basement, passing the kitchen and pantry (which still has its ingenious rat-proof shelving) to reach the main living quarters on the ground level and parlour floor. Here you will find tasteful Georgian furniture and furnishings, paintings, and costumes of the period 1780–1820. The small details are captivating—the hastener (tea trolley) in the kitchen, the feather shaving brush in the gentleman's washing room, and the early exercise machine in the bedroom. Climb to the top floor to see the childrens' playroom with its collection of toys, and on the way up admire the wood carving of Napoleon by Bozzanigo Torino in the master bedroom. Don't miss the exquisite Waterford crystal chandelier and the fine Mount Mellick embroidery.

*Top & right: the Georgian era recaptured inside Number Twenty Nine*

## HIGHLIGHTS

- ● Wood carving of Napoleon
- ● Examples of Mount Mellick embroidery
- ● Playroom
- ● Waterford crystal chandelier

## INFORMATION

- ✚ M10; locator map F4
- ✉ 29 Lower Fitzwilliam Street
- ☎ 702 6165
- ⏰ Tue–Sat 10–5; Sun 2–5. Closed two weeks before Christmas
- 🍴 Café
- 🚇 Pearse
- 🚌 Cross-city buses
- 🚻 None
- 💷 Moderate
- ↔ Natural History Museum (► 47), National Gallery (► 48)
- ❓ Visit by guided tour only

# The Casino, Marino

## HIGHLIGHTS

- Geometrical design
- Corner lions
- Curving wooden doors
- Stucco work
- Marquetry floors

## INFORMATION

- ✚ Q1; locator map off F1
- ✉ Off the Malahide Road, Marino
- ☎ 833 1618
- 🕐 Feb, Mar, Nov, Dec: Sat, Sun noon–4; Apr: Sat, Sun noon–5; May, Oct: daily 10–5; Jun–Sep: daily 10–6. (Last admission 45 mins before closing)
- 🚆 Clontarf Road
- 🚌 20B, 27, 27C, 42, 42B, 43, 127, 129
- ♿ None
- 💰 Moderate
- ❓ Visit by guided tour only

*Exotic woods in a marquetry floor*

**Once described as "a flawless and perfectly cut diamond set into the emerald diadem that is Ireland," the Casino has to be the country's most compact and ingenious 18th-century architectural creation.**

**Inspiration** The Casino is now surrounded by modern suburbia. But when viewed in its original rural setting, this deceptively small building must have resembled a Roman temple in Elysian fields. Its enlightened patron was James Caulfield, fourth Viscount Charlemont (1728–99), whose travels in the Mediterranean inspired him to re-create classical elegance and ingenuity in his homeland. To achieve this, he enticed King George III's architect, Sir William Chambers (1723–96), to design three buildings on his lands. Two survive: the first is his town house, now home to the Hugh Lane Gallery (► 37), and the second is this delightful house whose name derives from the Italian word *casa*. Curiously, Chambers never came to Ireland to see his masterpiece.

**Geometry** Its floor plan is a Greek cross encircled by pillars on a raised podium with benign lions at each corner creating a diagonal axis. Columns are water pipes, urns are chimneys. What seems from the outside like a single interior space comprises 16 rooms. The four state rooms on the ground floor are perfect in detail—with curving wooden doors, stucco friezes illustrating musical instruments and agricultural implements, and marquetry floors carefully assembled with a variety of rare woods. The whole building was "carefully worked out to produce a totally homogeneous design full of both excitement and repose."

# DUBLIN's
## best

# Museums & Galleries

## ART IN TEMPLE BAR

This cultural quarter of the city has several excellent venues showing contemporary work by young artists.

**Arthouse Multimedia Centre**
Exhibitions and events in an eye-catching building.
➕ K9 ✉ Curved Street
☎ 605 6800 🕙 Mon–Fri 10–5 🚆 Tara Street
🚌 Cross-city buses

**Gallery of Photography**
Ireland's leading centre for contemporary photography.
➕ K9 ✉ Meeting House Square ☎ 671 4654

**Meeting House Square**
Open-air cinema and performance space for artists' work.
➕ K9 ✉ Temple Bar
🚆 Tara Street 🚌 Cross-city buses

*Whiskey galore! The bottling line at the Old Jameson Distillery*

## DOUGLAS HYDE GALLERY

Contemporary gallery providing a forum for talent from Ireland and overseas.
➕ L10 ✉ Trinity College, Nassau Street entrance ☎ 608 1116
🕙 Mon–Fri 11–6; Thu 11–7; Sat 11–4.45 🍴 Buttery Bar on campus
🚆 Pearse 🚌 Cross-city buses 🚹 Few 🎫 Free

## DUBLIN'S VIKING ADVENTURE

An interactive experience of Viking Dublin. You can walk the streets of the Viking town of "Dyflin," chat to locals, observe their daily work and experience the sounds and smells of the city. At the end of your tour you'll see displays of Viking finds excavated from a nearby site and a small laboratory equipped with the tools and materials to preserve the artefacts. At the time of writing the Viking Adventure was closed for renovation and is due to open for the 2003 season.
➕ H8 ✉ Essex Street West, Temple Bar ☎ 679 6040 🕙 Apr–Sep: Tue–Sat 10–4.30 🚆 Tara Street 🚌 51B, 78A, 121, 123 🚹 Good
🎫 Expensive

### IRISH JEWISH MUSEUM

The synagogue that opened here in 1918 is now a museum dedicated to the history of Ireland's Jewish community since the mid-19th century.

✚ Off H12  ✉ 4 Walworth Road, off Victoria Street  ☎ 676 0737
🕐 Oct–Apr: Sun only 10.30–2.30. May–Sep: Tue, Thu, Sun 11–3.30
🚌 19, 19A, 22, 22A  ♿ Few  💲 Free

### NATIONAL WAX MUSEUM

Brings to life everyone from Irish historical figures to the cult cartoon family the Simpsons. You'll find the obligatory Hall of the Megastars and Chamber of Horrors as well as a World of Fairytale and Fantasy.

✚ J6  ✉ Granby Row, Parnell Square  ☎ 872 6340  🕐 Mon–Sat 10–5.30; Sun noon–5.30
🍴 Coffee shop  🚌 11, 13A, 16A  ♿ Few  💲 Moderate

*Trophy of musical instruments (1725) in the organ case at St. Michan's Church—near the Old Jameson Distillery*

### OLD JAMESON DISTILLERY

Explore the history of Irish whiskey-making through exhibits and audio-visual presentations on the site of the old Jameson Distillery. Sample a drop of the *uisce beatha*, literally "water of life," at the visitor bar, which is included in the admission price. Guided tours only.

✚ G8  ✉ Bow Street, Smithfield  ☎ 807 2355  🕐 Daily 9–6.
Tours every 40 minutes  🍴 Restaurant, visitor bar  🚌 67, 67A, 68, 69, 79, 90  ♿ Good  💲 Expensive

### PEARSE MUSEUM

Former school run by Patrick Pearse, the Dublin-born poet and revolutionary executed in 1916 at Kilmainham Gaol (▶ 26).

✚ Of map  ✉ St. Edna's Park, Grange Road, Rathfarnham  ☎ 493 4208  🕐 Daily 10–1 and Nov–Jan: 2–4. Feb–Apr, Sep, Oct: 2–5. May–Aug: 2–5.30  🚌 16  🍴 Tea rooms  ♿ Ground floor  💲 Free

### RHA GALLAGHER GALLERY

Prestigious gallery with well-chosen exhibits by Irish and overseas artists. The annual late spring exhibition showcases the best in contemporary Irish art. There is also an attractive outdoor sculpture courtyard.

✚ L10  ✉ 15 Ely Place  ☎ 661 2558  🕐 Tue–Sat 11–5; Thu 11–8; Sun 2–5  🍴 Pearse  🚌 Cross-city buses  ♿ Good  💲 Free

### SHAW BIRTHPLACE

Full of Victorian charm, the childhood home of the playwright George Bernard Shaw (1856–1950) has been restored with great attention to detail.

✚ J11  ✉ 33 Synge Street  ☎ 475 0854 or 872 2077
🕐 May–Sep: Mon–Sat 10–5; Sun and public hols 2–6. Closed for tours 1–2  🚌 16, 19  ♿ Few  💲 Moderate (a combined ticket is available for Dublin Writers Museum and James Joyce Museum)

### WATERWORLD

Known to locals as "the box in the docks," the white cube in the middle of the Grand Canal basin houses the Waterways Visitors Centre. With the help of working and scale models, it traces the story of Ireland's inland waterways and their use for commerce and recreation.

✚ N9  ✉ Grand Canal Quay  ☎ 677 7510  🕐 Jun–Sep: daily 9.30–5.30. Oct–May: Wed–Sun 12.30–5  🚆 Grand Canal Dock  🚌 2, 3  💲 Inexpensive

# Georgian Dublin

*Fitzwilliam Square is lined with red-brick Georgian houses famed for their arched doorways*

## HISTORY

The architectural style of Dublin's magnificent Georgian buildings developed during the reign of kings George I–IV, who occupied the English throne from 1714–1830. During this period, the city was planned and laid out with wide boulevards, spacious squares, and terraces of elegant town houses. Notable architects were James Gandon, Edward Lovett Pearce, Francis Johnston, Richard Cassels, Robert Parke, Thomas Cooley, and William Chambers. Most public buildings are still in use, although visitor access may be restricted.

---

### In the Top 25

**19 BANK OF IRELAND (► 40)**
**25 THE CASINO, MARINO (► 50)**
**14 GENERAL POST OFFICE (► 39)**
**9 MARSH'S LIBRARY (► 34)**
**17 NEWMAN HOUSE (► 42)**
**24 NUMBER TWENTY NINE (► 49)**

---

### CUSTOM HOUSE

Designed by James Gandon in 1791, the Custom House (► 22) is an outstanding example of Georgian architecture. The visitor centre has a museum with displays on Gandon's work and the building's history.
➕ L7 ✉ Custom House Quay ☎ 888 2538 🕐 Mid-Mar to Nov: Mon–Fri 10–12.30; Sat–Sun 2–5. Nov to mid-Mar: Wed–Fri 10–12.30; Sun 2–5 🚊 Tara Street 🚌 Cross-city buses ♿ Good 💷 Inexpensive

### FITZWILLIAM SQUARE

Surrounded by tall elegant buildings, this is one of Dublin's most famous Georgian squares, now given over mostly to offices, and apartments. Residents have keys to the gardens.
➕ L11 🚌 Cross-city buses 💷 Free

### FOUR COURTS

Home to the Irish law courts since 1796, the Four Courts (► 22) has much in common with the Custom House—primarily its designer, James Gandon. The building also suffered fire damage (as did the Custom House) during the turbulent events of 1921. You can visit only when courts are in session.
➕ G8 ✉ Inns Quay ☎ 886 6000 🚌 Cross-city buses
♿ Few 💷 Free

### GANDON'S RIVER BUILDINGS (➤ 22)

### KING'S INNS
The honorable society of the King's Inns is the impressive setting for Dublin law students training for the bar. Steeped in tradition, this beautiful building was begun by James Gandon. Tours by prior arrangement.
➕ H6 ✉ Henrietta Street ☎ 874 4840 🚌 25, 25A, 66, 67, 90 ♿ Few 🎫 Free

### LEINSTER HOUSE
Leinster House is the seat of Irish government and home to Dáil Éireann (House of Representatives) and Senead Éireann (Senate). You can visit by prior arrangement when parliament is not in session.
➕ L9 ✉ Kildare Street ☎ 618 3000 🚆 Pearse 🚌 Cross-city buses ♿ Good 🎫 Free

### MANSION HOUSE
The official residence of the Lord Mayor of Dublin since 1715. In 1919, the first parliament of the Irish people met here to adopt Ireland's Declaration of Independence from Britain. Closed to visitors.
➕ K10 ✉ Dawson Street 🚆 Pearse 🚌 Cross-city buses

### MERRION SQUARE
The best preserved Georgian square in Dublin and, as the wall plaques testify, home to many historical Irish figures including Daniel O'Connell and William Butler Yeats. The public park is a hidden gem, well worth exploring after a visit to Number Twenty Nine (➤ 49).
➕ L10 🚆 Pearse 🚌 Cross-city buses 🎫 Free

### THE OSCAR WILDE HOUSE
On the north side of Merrion Square is the house where Oscar Wilde lived from 1855 to 1876. It was the first house to be built in the square in 1762 and is an excellent example of Georgian architecture
➕ L9 ✉ 1 Merrion Square ☎ 662 0281 🕐 Mon, Wed, Thu tours at 10.15, 11.15 🚆 Pearse 🚌 Cross-city buses ♿ No disabled access 🎫 Inexpensive

### ROYAL COLLEGE OF SURGEONS
One of Dublin's later Georgian constructions, this jewel of a building on the northwest corner of St. Stephen's Green, dates from 1806 and was designed by architect Edward Parke. Contact Terry Slattery, Head Porter, in advance to arrange a personal tour.
➕ J10 ✉ St. Stephen's Green ☎ 402 2263 🚌 Cross-city buses ♿ Few 🎫 Free

### GEORGIAN HOUSES

Dublin's Georgian houses were built to a basic harmonious design. They generally have five storeys and, typically, pillars and wrought-iron railings, panelled front doors, fanlights, and side windows, all combining to create an external symmetry. Inside, the spacious, high-ceilinged rooms are often embellished with elegant stucco work, wood panelling, and marble fireplaces.

*An elegant Georgian doorway in Fitzwilliam Square with typical gossamer fanlight above*

# Gardens & Parks

## DUBLIN'S SECRET GARDEN

Only a 10-minute walk from O'Connell Street, at the end of Blessington Street, is the former city reservoir, Blessington Street Basin. Here you will find a quiet haven of peace for visitors and local wildlife. Landscaped in the mid-1990s it remains largely undiscovered and has become known as Dublin's secret garden. Open seven days a week during daylight hours, you can reach it on a No. 10 bus.

### IVEAGH GARDENS

One of Dublin's finest yet least well-known parks. Designed in 1863, these secluded gardens shelter a rustic grotto, cascade fountains, maze, archery grounds, wilderness, and woodlands.

➕ J11 ✉ Clonmel Street ☎ 475 7816 🚌 Cross-city buses 🎫 Free

### PHOENIX PARK

A vast expanse of green space, lakes, and woodland in the heart of the city, this is the largest urban park in Europe, covering some 696ha (1,720 acres) and encircled by an 13km (8-mi) wall. Within its confines are Dublin Zoo (➤ 57), the American Ambassador's home, and the Irish President's residence, *Áras an Uachtaráin*. The visitor centre, where you'll find a lively exhibition about the park, is on the site of the old Papal Nunciature, near the Phoenix Monument.

➕ A7 🚌 37, 38, 39 (Parkgate Street entrance) 🎫 Visitor centre: inexpensive; park: free

### ST. STEPHEN'S GREEN

A hugely popular place when the sun comes out, this park in the centre of the city was originally common land used for public hangings, among other activities. By 1880, it had become a public garden, thanks to the benevolence of Lord Ardilaun, a member of the Guinness family. Listen for lunchtime concerts and gigs on the bandstand in summer.

➕ K10 🚆 Pearse 🚌 Cross-city buses 🎫 Free

### WAR MEMORIAL GARDENS

These wonderful gardens are dedicated to the 49,400 Irish soldiers who died in World War I. Especially moving are the thousands of names etched in the granite book rooms and the beautiful sunken rose gardens. Rowers can sometimes be seen gliding along the River Liffey. Well off the tourist beat.

➕ A9 ✉ Islandbridge ☎ 677 0236 🚌 25, 25A, 26, 28, 68, 69 🎫 Free

*Ducks on the pond expect to be fed by the Dubliners who come in their droves to relax in the peaceful city-centre surroundings of St. Stephen's Green*

# Children's Activities

### DUBLIN ZOO

More than 700 animals from around the globe live in 24ha (60 acres) of landscaped grounds among the ornamental lakes of Dublin Zoo, many with plenty of room to roam. Visit Monkey Island, the Arctic Fringes, and the World of the Primates, and don't miss the Pet Care Area, Reptile House, and Discovery Centre. Check out the newborn babies and feeding programmes.

⊞ B6 ⊠ Phoenix Park ☎ 677 1425 ⏰ Mar–Oct: Mon–Sat 9.30–6; Sun 10.30–6. Nov–Feb: Mon–Sat 9.30–dusk; Sun 10.30–dusk. Feeding times 11–3.45 🚌 10 🍴 Restaurant, cafés ♿ Good 💶 Expensive

*Children's favourite at Dublin Zoo*

### FRY MODEL RAILWAY

In the grounds of Malahide Castle (➤ 20), this is a unique collection of handmade models of Irish trains, from the beginning of rail travel to the present day. A great family day out.

⊞ Off map, 13km (8 miles) from Dublin ⊠ Malahide Castle Demesne, Malahide ☎ 846 3779 ⏰ Apr–Sep: Mon–Sat 10–5 🚉 Connolly Station to Malahide 🚌 42 ♿ Good 💶 Moderate

### PARNELL CENTRE (➤ 81)

### THE ARK

This specially created cultural centre for children offers around 10 programmes throughout the year with emphasis on art and culture for children aged 4–14 years.

⊞ h7 ⊠ Eustace Street ☎ 670 7788 🚉 Tara Street 🚌 Cross-city buses ♿ Good 💶 Depends on activity

### VIKING SPLASH TOURS

A most ingenious new tour where passengers are driven through Viking Dublin on amphibious buses before driving into the Grand Canal to finish the tour on water. Fun, educational, and exciting.

⊞ f9 ⊠ Bull Alley Street ☎ Recorded info 855 3000; reservations 828 3773 ⏰ Mar–mid-Jun and Sep–Nov: Wed–Mon tours every 30 minutes 10–12, 1.30–5; Sun first tour 10.30 💶 Expensive

### FEEDING CHILDREN IN DUBLIN

Two excellent child-friendly restaurants that are worth checking out are: Milano, an upmarket, colourful, and popular pizza place with patient staff, proving a popular haunt with parents ⊞ K9 ⊠ Dawson Street ☎ 670 7744 🚉 Pearse 🚌 Cross-city buses and TGI Fridays, a new arrival on the Dublin restaurant scene that understands kids ⊞ K10 ⊠ St. Stephen's Green ☎ 670 7744 🚉 Pearse 🚌 Cross-city buses.

# Dublin from the DART

*Dublin's overground light train brings you speedily to and from the city*

**DART** DUBLIN AREA RAPID TRANS

## DALKEY

Only a few stops south on the DART and you'll find yourself in the attractive former fishing village of Dalkey. The setting of Flann O'Brien's novel *The Dalkey Archive* (1964), the village has long had literary associations. George Bernard Shaw lived here and more recently Maeve Binchey and Hugh Leonard. James Joyce set chapter two of *Ulysses* in Dalkey. The Heritage Centre is accessed through Goat Castle in Castle Street and from the battlements you get a splendid view of the sea and mountains. Good pubs and restaurants enhance your visit.

## BLACKROCK (➤ 72)

## BRAY

In the early days of the Kingstown (Dun Laoghaire) Railway, Bray was a sophisticated seaside resort, known as the "Brighton of Ireland" after England's famous south coast community. Nowadays, this attractive seaside town, towards the southern end of the DART line, has become a playground for the young at heart who come for the amusements, bumper cars, and fortune-tellers operating on the promenade most of the year round. South County Dubliners come for the fine walks and splendid views around nearby Bray Head.

## DUN LAOGHAIRE

Invigorating walks along the piers at Dun Laoghaire, a Victorian seaside resort once known as Kingstown, are something of a Dublin institution. The scenery is stunning, and you can see the ferries plying to and fro across the Irish Sea. The East Pier has a bandstand, folk dancers, rollerbladers, and a busy stream of pedestrians. The longer West Pier on the other side is slightly rugged and attracts fishing enthusiasts. Walkers in search of warming hot toddies and chowder by an open fire will head for the Purty Kitchen pub nearby.

## HOWTH

This promontory to the north of Dublin is a traditional fishing village and trendy suburb in one. A popular sailing centre, the Howth marina is always packed with yachts from Ireland and abroad. Howth DART station is near the harbour and close to all the waterside activity, bars, and restaurants. Howth is idyllic in sunny weather, and is very busy over the Easter holiday when the place buzzes during one of Ireland's major jazz festivals. Check out the attractive castle grounds and Transport Museum (☎ 832 0427 for opening times).

### KILLINEY

National and international celebrities such as Bono, Damon Hill, Neil Jordan, and Eddie Irvine have settled in the resort known affectionately as Dublin's Riviera. Killiney's distinctly Mediterranean feel is reflected in the names of the magnificent houses, such as La Scala, San Elmo, and Mount Etna. Take a walk along the Vico Road for what is arguably the most breathtaking view in Dublin. Look out to Dalkey Island, a craggy piece of land captured by the Vikings and later the site of Christian communities. Fishermen in nearby Coliemore Harbour run boat trips in summer to view the resident goats, ruined oratory, and Martello Tower.

### SANDYCOVE

James Joyce chose the Martello Tower along the sea front as the setting for the first chapter of *Ulysses* and the museum inside (☎ 280 9265 for opening times) displays some of his letters, books, photographs, and personal possessions. A bracing swim may introduce you to other die-hards who take the plunge all year around. Once gentlemen-only (and nudist to boot!), Sandycove beach is now used by swimmers of both sexes—with suits. Although the DART seems to veer away from the shore at Sydney Parade, it's just a five-minute walk to Sandymount Strand, popular with joggers and dog owners. After work, Dubliners come here to chill out. There are good views across to Howth and the north side of Dublin.

### VIEWS FROM THE DART

- Dalkey Island off Killiney
- Sailboats off Dun Laoghaire
- Blackrock's public park and private gardens
- Wetlands bird sanctuary at Booterstown
- Custom House between Tara Street and Connolly Station
- Urban jungle of Kilbarrack, backdrop for novels *The Commitments*, *The Snapper*, and *The Van*, Roddy Doyle's prize-winning trilogy

*Howth village and harbour*

# Traditional Irish Entertainment

*O'Donoghue's singing pub in Merrion Row*

### A DUBLIN INSTITUTION

O'Donoghue's is an authentic old pub where traditional Irish music is spontaneous and lively. Small and intimate, it gets very crowded with tourists and locals. It's a magnet for musicians playing anything from a fiddle or *bodhrán* to accordian or spoons. The folk group The Dubliners started their career here is the early 1960s.

### BURLINGTON CABARET
Nightly cabaret from May to October. Acknowledged rival to Jurys Cabaret (▶ below).
✚ Off L12 ✉ Burlington Hotel, Upper Leeson Street ☎ 664 3186
🚌 11, 11A, 13B, 46A

### INTERNATIONAL BAR
Indulge in a hefty helping of Irish wit at the home of the Comedy Cellar, founded by comic geniuses Ardal O'Hanlon, Dylan Moran, and others. The daily evening programme of events encompasses blues and country music as well as comedy.
✚ j8 ✉ 23 Wicklow Street ☎ 677 9250 🚉 Pearse
🚌 Cross-city buses

### JURYS CABARET
A hugely popular venue for comedy, music, song, and dance from May to October. Book ahead for the show, with or without dinner.
✚ Off P12 ✉ Jurys Hotel, Pembroke Road, Ballsbridge ☎ 660 5000
🚉 Lansdowne Road 🚌 5, 7, 7A, 8, 45

### OLIVER ST. JOHN GOGARTY
A pub since the mid-19th century, Gogarty's stands in the heart of Temple Bar and is a very popular venue for traditional music and dance. Good food, good *craic*, and a great night out.
✚ J8 ✉ 58–59 Fleet Street ☎ 671 1822 ⊙ Music daily 2PM–1.30AM 🚉 Tara Street 🚌 Cross-city buses

### O'SHEA'S MERCHANT
Nightly traditional music and dancing—everyone is encouraged to take to the dance floor.
✚ G8 ✉ 12 Lower Bridge Street ☎ 679 6793 🚌 21, 21A

### TAYLORS THREE ROCK
Enjoy an Irish night out with a banquet and traditional music and dancing. Top ballad groups appear all year. Expect audience participation! Advance booking.
✚ Off map ✉ Grange Road, Rathfarnham ☎ 494 2999 🚌 16C, 48A (and 5–10-minute walk). Ask at tourist information for directions

# Rock Heritage

### BAD ASS CAFÉ

Long-established pizza restaurant that once employed a young Sinead O'Connor as a waitress.
✚ h7  ✉ 9 Crown Alley, Temple Bar
☎ 671 2596  🚉 Tara Street
🚌 Cross-city buses

### CAPTAIN AMERICA'S COOKHOUSE

Singer-songwriter Chris De Burgh, of *Lady in Red* fame, got his first live break in this uninspiring burger restaurant. Lots of rock memorabilia.
✚ j9  ✉ 44 Grafton Street  ☎ 671 5266  🚉 Pearse  🚌 Cross-city buses

### GRESHAM HOTEL

Once Dublin's grandest hotel, steeped in history. In the 1960s, the Beatles played an impromptu session here, the band's only live performance in Ireland. The forming of the Chieftains, Ireland's greatest exponents of traditional music, also happened here in the 1960s.
✚ k6  ✉ 23 Upper O'Connell Street  ☎ 874 6881  🚌 Cross-city buses

### KORKY'S SHOE SHOP

A young Ronan Keating fitted and sold fashionable shoes to trendy youngsters here before hitting the top of the charts with Boyzone.
✚ j9  ✉ Grafton Street  ☎ 670 7943  🚉 Pearse
🚌 Cross-city buses

### THE RED BOX

This was the venue where Westlife held some of their finest rehearsals. Originally called I.O.U., Westlife gradually took shape with replacements for the band found from auditions held at Red Box. It is still a popular dance venue.
✚ J11  ✉ Harcourt Street  ☎ 478 0225  🚉 Pearse  🚌 Cross-city buses

### WINDMILL LANE STUDIOS

Fans still make pilgrimages to the recording and editing studios that nurtured U2 in the early days, before 1987, when their album "The Joshua Tree" brought them worldwide fame. Small groups gather wistfully outside and leave graffiti messages on the walls as a tribute to their heroes.
✚ Off map  ✉ 4 Windmill Lane, Sir John Rogerson's Quay  🚌 1, 3

*U2—Dublin's most famous band*

### STARS

Artists such as Phil Lynott, Rory Gallagher, and The Dubliners put Dublin on the musical map and their success was followed in the 1970s and 1980s by The Virgin Prunes and The Boomtown Rats. The following decade saw the emergence of Sinead O'Connor, the Hothouse Flowers, and Boyzone. Occupying centre stage is Dublin's greatest musical export—U2, formed in 1978. Check out the city's musical landmarks with the help of the booklet *Rock 'n Stroll— Dublin's Music Trail*, available from Dublin Tourism and many bookstores.

# Statues & Monuments

*Jakki McKenna's statue*
Meeting Place *is better*
*known as "The Hags*
*with the Bags"*

## NICKNAMES

Political correctness is cast aside in Dublin-speak when referring to the city's sculptures. The Anna Livia fountain which used to be on O'Connell Street, symbolizing the River Liffey, and known by all as the "Floozie in the Jacuzzi" is still to be relocated. Locals have dubbed the statue of Molly Malone as the "Tart with the Cart." Meanwhile, the Dublin shoppers at the north end of the Ha'penny Bridge (see picture above) are the "Hags with the Bags."

## BRASS FOOTPRINTS
Three sets of brass footprints can be found on the way from Westmoreland Street to O'Connell Bridge. This quirky urban art is from the young multimedia artist, Rachel Joynt.
🕂 J6 ✉ O'Connell Bridge 🚉 Tara Street 🚌 Cross-city buses

## CHILDREN OF LÍR
A poignant Irish fairy tale, about three children turned into swans by a wicked stepmother, inspired Oisín Kelly's bronze sculpture (1971). It is the focal point of this garden, dedicated to those who died in pursuit of Irish independence.
🕂 J6 ✉ Garden of Remembrance, Parnell Square East ☎ 874 3074 🚌 Cross-city buses

## FAMINE FIGURES
A series of emaciated figures along the quays commemorates the Great Famine of 1845–49. Plaques bearing the names of families who suffered will be added over time. (The sculptor, Rowan Gillespie, is also behind the "Spiderman" character scaling the Treasury Building on Grand Canal Street.)
🕂 L7 ✉ Custom House Quay 🚉 Tara Street 🚌 Cross-city buses

## FUSILIERS' ARCH
Also known as Traitors' Arch, this piece on the north-west corner of St. Stephen's Green is a tribute to the members of the Royal Dublin Fusiliers killed during the Boer War.
🕂 K10 ✉ St. Stephen's Green 🚉 Pearse 🚌 Cross-city buses

## MOLLY MALONE
The fishmonger of song is believed to have lived in Dublin until her death in 1734.
🕂 J8 ✉ Lower Grafton Street 🚉 Pearse 🚌 Cross-city buses

## OSCAR WILDE
This languid life-size figure of the famous writer, reclining on a rock at the northwest corner of Merrion Square, is especially haunting at night.
🕂 L9 ✉ Merrion Square 🚉 Pearse 🚌 Cross-city buses

## PATRICK KAVANAGH
Sit and watch the swans slip by with the bronze of poet Patrick Kavanagh (1905–67), who loved this piece of leafy calm in the heart of commercial Dublin.
🕂 M11 ✉ Grand Canal, near Baggot Street Bridge 🚌 10

# DUBLIN
# where to...

## EAT

## SHOP

## BE ENTERTAINED

## STAY

# Elegant Dining

## PRICES

Approximate prices for a two-course meal for one person with one drink:

| € | under €20 |
|---|---|
| €€ | €20–€45 |
| €€€ | above €45 |

## THINGS TO KNOW

• Eating out is extremely popular in Dublin, so book ahead. Many restaurants have terraces; these are open in fine weather. Some restaurants close on Monday.

• Most serious restaurants offer a fixed-price lunch menu that represents excellent value.

• A service charge of 12.5 percent is generally added and many diners add a tip of about 5 to 10 percent of the bill. If service is not included, a tip of 12.5–15 percent is usual.

• The restaurants are open for lunch and dinner seven days a week unless otherwise indicated.

### THE COMMONS (€€€)

A spacious dining room, decorated in Georgian style, in the lower ground floor of Newman House (► 42). The menu showcases creative combinations of the finest Irish produce. Stunning terrace.

✚ K10 ✉ 86 St. Stephen's Green ☎ 478 0530 🕐 Lunch Mon–Fri, dinner Mon–Sat 🚌 Cross-city buses

### LE COQ HARDI (€€€)

Politicians and captains of industry appreciate the genteel formality and discreet service in charmingly appointed rooms. An impressive wine cellar complements the excellent food.

✚ Off N12 ✉ 35 Pembroke Road, Ballsbridge ☎ 668 9070 🕐 Lunch Mon–Fri, dinner Mon–Sat 🚊 Lansdowne Road 🚌 5, 7, 7A, 8, 45

### L'ECRIVAIN (€€€)

With a refurbishment in January 2000, chef Derry Clarke's popular Irish modern restaurant continues to grow in stature. Friendly service.

✚ M11 ✉ 109a Lower Baggot Street ☎ 661 1919 🕐 Lunch Mon–Fri, dinner Mon–Sat 🚌 10

### FADO (€€€)

Next door to the Lord Mayor's official residence, the spacious dining room is set in the resplendent bell epoque era. A friendly staff serves modern Irish food with a hint of Mediterranean and Asian influences.

✚ e4 ✉ The Mansion House, Dawson Street ☎ 676 7200

🕐 Lunch and dinner Mon–Sat 🚌 Cross-city buses

### LANYONS (€€€)

Excellent service and lavish surroundings ensure a memorable dining experience. The contemporary Irish cooking combines fine traditional dishes with exciting new trends.

✚ L9 ✉ The Davenport Hotel, Merrion Square ☎ 607 3500 🕐 Lunch and dinner daily 🚊 Pearse 🚌 Cross-city buses

### LES FRÈRES JACQUES (€€€)

Excellent French cooking in a stylish but informal setting. The friendly owner and staff are happy to offer advice on the exquisite menu and wines. Centrally located.

✚ c2 ✉ 74 Dame Street ☎ 679 4555 🕐 Lunch Mon–Fri, dinner Mon–Sat 🚌 Cross-city buses

### PEACOCK ALLEY (€€€)

Eclectic cuisine created by trend-setting *wunderkind* Conrad Gallagher, using the best ingredients in exciting new combinations.

✚ j10 ✉ Fitzwilliam Hotel, St. Stephen's Green West ☎ 478 7015 🕐 Lunch Tue–Fri, dinner daily 🚊 Pearse 🚌 Cross-city buses

### RESTAURANT PATRICK GUILBAUD (€€€)

Superlative cuisine by French chef Patrick Guilbaud. Tastefully decorated, with a wonderful collection of Irish art.

✚ L10 ✉ Merrion Hotel, 21 Upper Merrion Street ☎ 676 4192 🕐 Lunch, dinner Tue–Sat 🚊 Pearse 🚌 Cross-city buses

# Trend Setters

### BANG CAFÉ (€€)

Cool and minimal, Bang is as trendy and fresh as its get-ahead clientele. The eclectic, modern menu is as fashionable as its cosmopolitan interiors.

➕ L10 ✉ Merrion Row ☎ 675 0898 🚇 Pearse 🚌 Cross-city buses

### BRASSERIE NA MARA (€€€)

A sophisticated, deceptively grand restaurant, frequented by well-heeled locals and the expense account set. The emphasis is on fresh, local seafood.

➕ Off map ✉ The Harbour, Dun Laoghaire ☎ 280 6767 🕐 Lunch Mon–Fri, dinner Mon–Sat 🚇 Dun Laoghaire 🚌 7, 7A, 8

### BRUNO'S (€€)

The splendid fusion of Irish favourites with Mediterranean and French flavours attracts a hip clientele. Modern and airy.

➕ c2 ✉ 30 East Essex Street ☎ 670 6767 🕐 Lunch Mon–Fri, dinner Mon–Sat 🚇 Tara Street 🚌 Cross-city buses

### COOKE'S CAFÉ (€€)

When it opened in 1992, Cooke's broke new ground in terms of decor and cuisine. The menu, with California and Italian influences, includes Caesar salad, angel hair pasta, and delicious pecan pie.

➕ c3 ✉ 14 South William Street ☎ 679 0536 🚇 Pearse 🚌 Cross-city buses

### EDEN (€€)

Contemporary restaurant with predominantly white decor and floor-to-ceiling windows, serving modern Irish food with a Mediterranean slant. Popular on summer evenings and for Sunday lunch when the Temple Bar market is in full swing outside.

➕ c2 ✉ Meeting House Square ☎ 670 5372 🚇 Tara Street 🚌 Cross-city buses

### FITZERS (€€)

The most fashionable branch of the popular chain. Busy, fiery Mediterranean menu plus chunky burgers and fries.

➕ e4 ✉ 51 Dawson Street ☎ 677 1155 🚇 Pearse 🚌 Cross-city buses

### MAO (€€)

Colourful place with very modern food and Warholesque lithographs. No reservations, but tables turn quickly.

➕ c/d4 ✉ 2–3 Chatham Row ☎ 670 4899 🚇 Pearse 🚌 Cross-city buses

### MERMAID CAFÉ (€€)

Traditional Irish fare served in a contemporary minimalist style. Popular with those lured by the purest ingredients and tasty dishes like the excellent crab cakes.

➕ c2 ✉ 60–70 Dome Street ☎ 670 8236 🚌 Cross-city buses

### SIDE DOOR (€€)

Modern restaurant in Dublin's most traditional hotel. Colourful menu, from fish and chips to creatively topped pizzas.

➕ c5 ✉ Shelbourne Hotel, St. Stephen's Green ☎ 676 6471 🚇 Pearse 🚌 Cross-city buses

### IN VOGUE

Dublin's reputation as a fashionable youth-orientated city is borne out by the capital's cosmopolitan restaurant scene. Listed on these pages are the city's most popular haunts and you should make reservations as far ahead as possible. Many of Dublin's trendier restaurants have two evening seatings on weekends. The early seating is usually around 7PM while the later seating is from approximately 9.30PM. If you want to linger, be sure your table is not booked for a second party.

# International Cuisine

## CELTIC COOKING

Today's Irish cooking draws inspiration from many sources but simplicity is the key when it comes to serving fresh local produce. Smoked salmon, oysters, hearty soups, and stews are readily available in most Dublin restaurants and pubs, sometimes accompanied by soda bread, a dense yeast-free loaf that goes well with traditional dishes. Irish restaurants come in many guises: some adopt a traditional style serving comfort food, such as seafood chowder and Irish stew, in settings with turf fires and local music, while others are culinary trend setters nationally and internationally. If you would like to sample some of this authentic Irish cooking try Gallaghers Boxty (► below)

### GALLAGHERS BOXTY HOUSE (€€)

Traditional food focused around the boxty, an Irish potato pancake. Try the brown bread ice cream.
✚ d2 ✉ 20–21 Temple Bar ☎ 677 2762 🚇 Tara Street 🚌 Cross-city buses

## ASIAN

### AYA (€€)

Dublin's hippest conveyor sushi bar and restaurant, just off Grafton Street. Fun atmosphere.
✚ d3 ✉ Clarendon Street ☎ 677 1544 🕐 Lunch and dinner daily 🚇 Pearse 🚌 Cross-city buses

### CHILI CLUB (€€)

Small Thai restaurant selling tasty food.
✚ d4 ✉ 1 Anne's Lane, off South Anne's Street ☎ 677 3721 🕐 Lunch and dinner Mon–Sat 🚇 Pearse 🚌 Cross-city buses

### DIEP LE SHAKER (€)

A stylish haunt offering some of the best, beautifully presented Thai cuisine in Ireland. Sophisticated surroundings with a vibrant atmosphere.
✚ L10 ✉ 55 Pembroke Lane ☎ 661 1829 🕐 Lunch Mon–Fri, dinner Mon–Sat 🚇 Lansdowne Road 🚌 Cross-city buses

### EASTERN TANDOORI (€€)

Well known for its range of authentic dishes.
✚ c4 ✉ 34–35 South William Street ☎ 671 0506 🕐 Lunch Mon–Sat, dinner daily 🚇 Pearse 🚌 Cross-city buses

### IMPERIAL (€)

A family-run business established in Dublin since 1985, boasting some of the best Chinese cooking in the city.
✚ d3 ✉ 13 Wicklow Street ☎ 677 2580 🚇 Pearse 🚌 Cross-city buses

### LANGKAWI (€€)

Excellent Malaysian restaurant with an exciting, extensive menu. Totally tasty food that's high on flavour.
✚ N11 ✉ 46 Upper Baggot Street ☎ 668 2760 🕐 Lunch Mon–Fri, dinner Mon–Sat 🚇 Lansdowne Road 🚌 10

### RAJDOOT TANDOORI (€€€)

Dependable North Indian food, excellent service, and pleasant surroundings.
✚ d4 ✉ Westbury Hotel, Clarendon Street ☎ 679 4274 🕐 Lunch Mon–Sat, dinner daily 🚇 Pearse 🚌 Cross-city buses

### SHALIMAR (€€)

Innovative cooking from the different regions of India is served in the formal candlelit restaurant, while downstairs the open kitchen setting offers simple balti dishes.
✚ c3 ✉ 17 South Great Georges Street ☎ 677 3478 🕐 Lunch and dinner daily 🚇 Pearse 🚌 Cross-city buses

### WAGAMAMA (€€)

Fast and furious woks churn out healthy substantial Japanese dishes in a minimalist environment.
✚ d5 ✉ St. Stephen's Green Shopping Centre, South King Street ☎ 478 2152 🚇 Pearse 🚌 Cross-city buses

### YAMAMORI NOODLES (€€)

Japanese noodle and sushi house frequented by young Dubliners.
✚ c3 ✉ 71–72 South Great Georges Street ☎ 475 5001 🚌 Cross-city buses

## EUROPEAN

### BELGO (€€)

Spacious, high-ceilinged Belgian restaurant famous for its mussel dishes and more than 100 varieties of Belgian beer.

✚ c2 ✉ 17–18 Sycamore Street ☎ 672 7555 🕐 Lunch and dinner daily 🚇 Tara Street 🚌 Cross-city buses

### LA MÈRE ZOU (€€)

Contemporary eatery that prides itself on good Franco-Belgian cuisine. Ask about the good value "Big Plates."

✚ e5 ✉ 22 St. Stephen's Green ☎ 661 6669 🕐 Lunch daily 🚇 Pearse 🚌 Cross-city buses

### STEPS OF ROME (€)

Divine pizza by the slice plus other gutsy fare.

✚ d3 ✉ Chatham Street ☎ 670 5630 🚇 Pearse 🚌 Cross-city buses

### TRASTEVERE (€€)

Upbeat eatery that blends Italian food with a taste of New York. People-watch through the huge glass windows that front onto Temple Bar Square.

✚ c2 ✉ Unit 1 Temple Bar Square ☎ 679 7182 🕐 Lunch and dinner daily 🚇 Tara Street 🚌 Cross-city buses

### TRENTUNO (€€)

Colourful modern restaurant with varied menu offering huge portions of Italian dishes.

✚ d3 ✉ 31 Wicklow Street ☎ 677 4190 🚇 Pearse 🚌 Cross-city buses

### TZAR IVAN (€€)

This taste of Russia in the heart of Dublin creates a genuine Russian ambience and music enhances the atmosphere.

✚ j8 ✉ 30–31 Clarendon Street ☎ 671 6997 🕐 Lunch and dinner daily 🚇 Pearse 🚌 Cross-city buses

## OTHER FLAVOURS

### THE CEDAR TREE (€€)

Middle Eastern setting where tasty food centres around Lebanese dishes and *meze*. A belly dancer performs on Saturday nights.

✚ d3 ✉ 11 St. Andrew's Street ☎ 677 2121 🕐 Dinner only 🚇 Pearse 🚌 Cross-city buses

### BELLA CUBA (€€)

Flavoursome Cuban dishes served with a smile in a tropical atmosphere accompanied by salsa music. Cocktails.

✚ Off map ✉ 11 Ballsbridge Terrace ☎ 660 5539 🚇 Lansdowne Road 🚌 Cross-city buses

### MEXICO TO ROME (€€)

Unique menu allows you to mix favourite Mexicanos with Italian dishes. Busy and informal.

✚ c2 ✉ 23 East Essex Street ☎ 677 2727 🕐 Lunch and dinner daily 🚇 Tara Street 🚌 Cross-city buses

### NECTAR (€)

Airy, relaxed eatery renowned for refreshing and healthy Australian and international cuisine, juices and smoothies.

✚ c3 ✉ 7–9 Exchequer Street ☎ 672 7501 🕐 Lunch and dinner daily 🚇 Tara Street 🚌 Cross-city buses

### EXOTIC FLAVOURS

In Dublin today there has been a notable surge in the number of European, Eastern, and Far Eastern restaurants. French, Italian and Mediterranean fare, Scandinavian specialities, Russian, Indian, Japanese, and Oriental dishes—the choice from around the world is endless. Other restaurants with an international flavour include: **Acapulco** offering excellent Tex-Mex cooking ✉ 7 South Great Georges Street ☎ 677 1085; **Bahay Kubo** for unique Filipino cuisine such as *Sinigang Na Manok*—hot and sour chicken soup with chilli, lemon grass, and lime leaves ✉ 14 Bath Avenue, Sandymount ☎ 660 5572; **Marrakesh** with interesting Moroccan fare ✉ 28 South Anne's Street ☎ 679 4409; **Tante Zoe's** for Cajun/Creole cooking; you won't find better gumbos and jambalayas this side of the Mississippi ✉ 1a Crow Street, Temple Bar ☎ 679 4407.

# Vegetarian Fare & Seafood

## A GOOD CATCH

Fresh fish is plentiful in Dublin restaurants. Oysters, mussels, crab, prawns (shrimps), salmon, ray, mackerel, sole, whiting, and trout are all found in local waters. They work equally well when cooked plainly, to intensify the flavours, or incorporated into more elaborate dishes. For a truly Irish gastronomic experience, wash down a dozen fresh oysters with a glass of Guinness and mop up the salty juices with home-baked brown bread. Monday is the one day of the week when the choice of fresh fish is limited. In Ireland, fishermen still take a rest on Sunday, so there are no deliveries the following day.

## FISH 'N' CHIPS

These are still a great traditional favourite in Dublin and a good value substantial meal. Among the classics are **Leo Burdock's** (✉ 2 Werburgh Street ☎ 454 0306) near Christ Church Cathedral where excellent fish and chips can be eaten across the road in the cathedral garden. Another institution is **Beshoff** (✉ 14 Westmoreland Street ☎ 677 8025), a much loved fixture of Dublin since 1913 with good-size portions served in an attractive dining room.

## BLAZING SALADS (€)

Interesting salads and vegetarian fare. Popular with shoppers.
✚ c3 ✉ 21c Powerscourt Townhouse Centre, Clarendon Street ☎ 671 9552 🕐 Lunch and snacks until 5.30 Mon–Sat 🚋 Pearse 🚌 Cross-city buses

## CAVISTONS (€€)

Immensely popular restaurant that arose from the success of the neighbouring shop. Fashionable fresh food with a Mediterranean slant.
✚ Off map ✉ 59 Glasthule Road, Sandycove ☎ 280 9245 🕐 Lunch until 6 Tue–Sat 🚋 Sandycove & Glasthule 🚌 59

## CORNUCOPIA (€)

Long-established city-centre vegetarian restaurant and shop with optional takeout service.
✚ d3 ✉ 19 Wicklow Street ☎ 677 7583 🕐 Breakfast, lunch, and dinner Mon–Sat 🚋 Pearse 🚌 Cross-city buses

## GUINEA PIG (THE FISH RESTAURANT) (€€€)

Family-run restaurant, adorned with rustic brass ornaments and decorative plates, with an extensive, though not exclusively, seafood-based menu.
✚ Off map ✉ 17 Railway Road, Dalkey ☎ 285 9055 🕐 Dinner only 🚋 Dalkey 🚌 59

## JUICE (€)

Vegetarian food and juice bar with a globally inspired menu that includes Japanese, Italian, Mexican, and Caribbean dishes.
✚ c4 ✉ 73–83 South Great Georges Street ☎ 475 7856 🚌 Cross-city buses

## KING SITRIC (€€€)

The fish are landed just a few yards from Dublin's most regal seafood restaurant. Popular with Dublin high society and visting gastronomes. Wonderful menu and wine cellar.
✚ Off map ✉ East Pier, Howth ☎ 832 5235 🕐 Lunch Mon–Fri, dinner Mon–Sat 🚋 Howth 🚌 31, 31B

## LORD EDWARD (€€€)

Dublin's oldest seafood restaurant serves a wide range of fish dishes, from Galway Bay oysters to Sole Véronique in traditional surroundings.
✚ a3 ✉ 22 Christchurch Place ☎ 454 2420 🕐 Lunch Mon–Fri, dinner Mon–Sat 🚌 Cross-city buses

## OCEAN (€)

Glass surrounded bar and restaurant with marvellous waterside view. The menu offers delicate portions of fresh shellfish and seafood along with wraps and salads. Perfect for sunny summer lunches.
✚ M9 ✉ Grand Canal Basin ☎ 668 8862 🕐 Lunch, dinner Mon–Sun 🚋 Grand Canal Dock 🚌 3

## PIER 32 (€€)

Exciting choices in a casual, nautical setting emphasizing the fish dishes on the broad menu. Everything is super-fresh and authentic
✚ L11 ✉ 23 Upper Pembroke Street ☎ 676 1494 🕐 Lunch Mon–Fri, dinner Mon–Sat 🚌 10, 13, 46A, 46B

# Casual Dining

### COCOON (€)
Modern, chic, and sleek, this hotel lobby-style bar serves champagne and fries in equal quantities to Dublin's smart snackers.
➕ e4 ✉ Royal Hibernian Way ☎ 679 6259 🕐 Food served at lunch only 🚇 Pearse 🚌 Cross-city buses

### DOCKERS (€)
Basic quayside pub frequented by old-style Dubliners as well as actors, film folk, and musicians. Made fashionable by the likes of U2 and Jim Sheridan, this is one of the city's best places for sausage sandwiches and pints of Guinness.
➕ N8 ✉ 5 Sir John Rogerson's Quay ☎ 677 1692 🕐 Food served at lunch only 🚌 1, 3, 53A

### EDDIE ROCKETS (€)
US-style diners offering burgers, fries, hot dogs, buffalo wings, and shakes with sassy service to anthems from a 1950s jukebox. Open from breakfast until midnight during the week, until the wee hours Thu–Sat. Branches city-wide. Check the telephone directory for your nearest.

### THE GLOBE (€)
Delicious home-made soup and sandwiches from Cooke's Café (➤ 65), and a mouth-watering array of pastries.
➕ c3 ✉ 11 South Great Georges Street ☎ 671 1220 🚌 Cross-city buses

### INKWELL BAR (€)
The bar in this small hotel is like a sitting room, and there are tables outside in summer. Tasty sandwiches and hearty specials all day.
➕ N10 ✉ Schoolhouse Hotel, Northumberland Road ☎ 667 5014 🕐 Food served at lunch only 🚇 Lansdowne Road 🚌 5, 7A, 45, 46

### KEOGHS (€)
Ideal for those informal nights out—whether a pre-theatre meal or a late-night feast. Friendly staff serves rustic Mediterranean cooking complemented by a good wine list.
➕ d2 ✉ 1–2 Trinity Street ☎ 677 8599 🕐 Dinner Wed–Sat 🚇 Pearse 🚌 Cross-city buses

### PASTA FRESCA (€)
A constantly fast-moving haunt dishing up excellent pasta and pizzas late into the evening.
➕ d3 ✉ 3–4 Chatham Street ☎ 679 2402 🕐 Lunch and dinner daily 🚇 Pearse 🚌 Cross-city buses

### THE SHACK (€€)
A cosy Temple Bar restaurant offering wholesome dishes using the best fresh ingredients.
➕ c2 ✉ 24 East Essex Street ☎ 679 0043 🕐 Lunch and dinner daily 🚇 Tara Street 🚌 Cross-city buses

### THOMAS READ (€)
Brasserie with an extensive menu of imaginative, freshly prepared home-style dishes. One of the best pub lunches in Dublin.
➕ b2 ✉ 1–4 Parliament Street ☎ 671 7283 🕐 Food served at lunch only 🚌 Cross-city buses

### PUB GRUB
Pubs in Dublin are synonymous with drinking, Guinness, traditional Irish music, and good *craic*. But pub food is becoming increasingly popular and, particularly for those on a limited budget, good value. You can get some excellent hearty meals, including traditional Irish stews, the boxty (Potato pancake), and colcannon (cabbage and potato). There is often a carvery with a choice of salads. Sample any of these accompanied by a pint of Guinness and you will be set up for an afternoon of sightseeing or shopping. Some of the best pubs for food include The Stag's Head (➤ 83) in Dame Court, The Brazen Head in Bridge Street Lower (➤ 83), The Lord Edward in Christchurch Place (➤ 68), O'Neills in Suffolk Street (➤ 83), and Oliver St. John Gogarty in Fleet Street in Temple Bar (➤ 60).

# Breakfast, Brunch & Snacks

## EARLY START

The traditional Irish breakfast consists of bacon, sausage, egg, mushrooms, tomato, black and white pudding (sausage-shaped meat product made from cows' blood and served in fried slices), and toast, washed down with strong tea or coffee. But few working Dubliners have time to indulge, except perhaps on weekends. Led by the power breakfast business community, more and more city dwellers are beginning to eat out first thing in the morning. New places are always opening or extending their menus, so keep an eye open.

## ALPHA RESTAURANT

Traditional café that serves all-day breakfast as well as huge mixed grills and snacks. Terrific for the morning after the night before.
✚ d3 ✉ Corner Wicklow Street and Clarendon Street ☎ 677 0213 🕔 Breakfast, lunch, and dinner Mon–Sat 🚉 Pearse 🚌 Cross-city buses

## CAFÉ IRIE

Laid-back, bohemian young café that is especially good for hearty breakfasts. Home-style snacks and big mugs of coffee keep diners going throughout the day.
✚ c2 ✉ 11 Fownes Street, Temple Bar ☎ 672 5090 🕔 Breakfast, lunch, and snacks Mon–Sat 🚉 Tara Street 🚌 Cross-city buses

## CAFÉ JAVA

Plenty for all tastes and appetites in both branches of this popular breakfast haunt. Frequent queues, but newspapers help pass the time.
✚ Off map; d4 ✉ 145 Upper Leeson Street; 5 South Anne's Street ☎ 660 0675; 670 7239 🕔 Breakfast and lunch 🚉 Pearse 🚌 11, 11A, 11B, 13, 46A, and cross-city buses

## CHOMPYS

Chompys is popular for its great American breakfast and brunch cooked to order and eaten on the balcony.
✚ d3 ✉ Powerscourt Shopping Centre, South William Street ☎ 679 4552 🚉 Pearse 🚌 Cross-city buses

## ELEPHANT AND CASTLE

Widest breakfast menu in Dublin with straight-forward American cuisine. Well worth the wait even when queues are long, particularly on Sundays.
✚ c/d2 ✉ 18 Temple Bar ☎ 679 3121 🕔 Breakfast, lunch and dinner 🚉 Tara Street 🚌 Cross-city buses

## EXPRESSO BAR

Matte black and chrome café-restaurant with two centrally located branches. Fashionable food, delicate pastries, and herbal teas.
✚ N11 ✉ St. Mary's Road ☎ 660 0585 🕔 Breakfast, lunch, and dinner 🚉 Lansdowne Road 🚌 5, 7A, 10, 45

## NUDE

Healthy fast food with an organic slant and the most creative combinations in wraps, salads, and smoothies.
✚ d3 ✉ 21 Suffolk Street ☎ 677 4804 🚉 Pearse 🚌 Cross-city buses

## ODESSA LOUNGE & GRILL

This 1970s-inspired restaurant attracts a hip clientele. A favourite for late Sunday brunch.
✚ c3 ✉ 13–14 Dame Court ☎ 670 7634 🕔 Brunch and dinner Sat, Sun, dinner Mon–Fri 🚉 Pearse 🚌 Cross-city buses

## TÁ SÉ MAHOGANÍ GASPIPES

Sunday brunch with newspapers and a menu that includes good vegetarian choices.
✚ F6 ✉ 17 Manor Street ☎ 679 8138 🚌 37, 39, 39A, 70

# Coffee & Afternoon Tea

### BEWLEY'S ORIENTAL CAFÉS

Wonderful tea, coffee, pastries, cakes, and buns, as well as traditional breakfasts and adequate cold lunches. Central branches stay open late (➤ side panel).

### BT2

Glass-fronted café in the BT2 store with great views of Grafton Street. Sit in white minimalist splendour nibbling tasty sandwiches, pastries, and salads or simply while away the afternoon over frothy coffees, hot chocolate, or fresh juices.
✚ d4 ✉ Grafton Street ☎ 679 5666 ext. 1200 🕐 Breakfast, lunch, and snacks 🚆 Pearse 🚌 Cross-city buses

### GLORIA JEANS

Everything for the coffee lover from high-tech paraphernalia to frothy double lattes. Sample the wide range of Arabica coffee beans that are available to buy.
✚ d3 ✉ Powerscourt Townhouse Centre, Clarendon Street ☎ 679 7772 🕐 Lunch, coffee, and snacks Mon–Sat 🚆 Pearse 🚌 Cross-city buses

### KAFFE MOCKA

A coffee house with over 50 types of coffee and an extensive menu of sandwiches, snacks, and tasty main dishes. Also newspapers, board games; library upstairs.
✚ c4 ✉ 39 South William Street ☎ 671 0978 🕐 Daily 8AM–4AM 🚆 Pearse 🚌 Cross-city buses

### METRO CAFÉ

Coffee, tea, hot chocolate, plus flavoursome light food. Newspapers too.
✚ c4 ✉ 43 South William Street ☎ 679 4515 🚆 Pearse 🚌 Cross-city buses

### QUEEN OF TARTS

Traditional tea shop offering a mouthwatering array of home-made cakes and savoury baking.
✚ b2 ✉ Cork Hill, Dame Street ☎ 670 7499 🕐 Daily 🚆 Tara Street 🚌 Cross-city buses

### SHELBOURNE HOTEL

The Lord Mayor's Lounge is the grandest of Dublin addresses for elegant afternoon tea with its dainty sandwiches, cakes, scones, and savoury morsels. Reserve ahead.
✚ e5 ✉ 27 St. Stephen's Green North ☎ 676 6471 🕐 Afternoon tea 3PM–5:30PM 🚆 Pearse 🚌 Cross-city buses

### WESTBURY HOTEL

Afternoon tea takes place in the large, open foyer, often accompanied by a pianist or fashion show.
✚ d4 ✉ Balfe Street, off Grafton Street ☎ 679 1122 🕐 Afternoon tea. Last orders 7PM 🚆 Pearse 🚌 Cross-city buses

### WINDING STAIR CAFÉ

Sip coffee at the top of a winding staircase within Dublin's loveliest bookshop overlooking the River Liffey. Good lunchtime snacks.
✚ c1 ✉ 40 Lower Ormond Quay ☎ 873 3292 🕐 Mon–Sat 🚆 Tara Street 🚌 Cross-city buses

### BEWLEY'S

Steeped in local history and folklore, Bewley's Oriental Cafés are a Dublin institution. The surroundings in the older premises (Westmoreland Street and Grafton Street) are glorious—old wooden panelled rooms, stained glass, vast coffee canisters. The banquettes are miraculously comfortable when you're settling in with your daily paper. Branches are at: 78 Grafton Street; 40 Mary Street; 10–12 Westmoreland Street and Santry.

# Shopping Centres & Department Store

## OUT OF TOWN

Outside the city, purpose-built shopping complexes incorporate high-street stores and individual speciality shops with leisure facilities to provide a convenient shopping experience.

Blanchardstown, a massive mall about a 20-minute drive northwest from town, has supermarkets, department stores, cinemas (➤ 81), and, more importantly, the best selection of price-wise and fashionable local and international retail names under one roof in the Dublin area.

The Liffey Valley shopping centre (a 20-minute drive southwest of the city) has over 90 retail outlets. The foodcourt has 12 restaurants and cafés including Eddie Rockets Diner and Spur Steakhouse. Ireland's largest cinema complex (➤ 81) is here with 14 screens. A retail park boasts many top names such as PC World and Motor World. Easy access by bus from the city.

Bargain hunters flock to Blackrock, 8km (5 miles) south of Dublin, for the market held every Saturday and Sunday, 10–5. Stalls sell clothes, bric-à-brac, crafts, and antiques. Easy to reach by bus and DART.

## ARNOTTS

This large department store stocks everything from the traditional to the fashionable in clothes, interiors, household, leisure, entertainment, and cosmetics.

➕ J7 ✉ Henry Street
☎ 805 0400 🚇 Tara Street
🚌 Cross-city buses

## AVOCA

One of Ireland's oldest surviving businesses, founded in 1723 and fast emerging as a fine department store for unique and exclusive high quality items combining the traditional with the fashionable. The splendid food hall is packed with Irish delicacies.

➕ j8 ✉ 11–13 Suffolk Street
☎ 677 4215 🚇 Pearse
🚌 Cross-city buses

## BROWN THOMAS

Ireland's stylish department store showcases Irish and international designer clothes. Also homeware, cosmetics, leather goods, accessories, and linens.

➕ K9 ✉ Grafton Street
☎ 605 6666 🚇 Pearse
🚌 Cross-city buses

## CLERY'S

A Dublin institution. Many romantic assignations have been made beneath the clock outside this department store. Refurbishment has brightened it up.

➕ K7 ✉ O'Connell Street,
☎ 878 6000 🚇 Tara Street
🚌 Cross-city buses

## ILAC CENTRE

Dublin's longest established shopping mall needs a face-lift. The labyrinth of smaller shops and a branch of Dunnes department store, centre around the County Library.

➕ J7 ✉ Henry Street
☎ 704 1460 🚇 Tara Street
🚌 Cross-city buses

## JERVIS CENTRE

You will find most British chain stores, including a huge Debenhams and Marks & Spencer at this modern shopping centre covering several floors. The upper floor is a vast foodcourt.

➕ J7 ✉ Jervis Street
☎ 878 1323 🚇 Tara Street
🚌 Cross-city buses

## POWERSCOURT TOWNHOUSE CENTRE

A warren of boutiques, gift and craft stores, restaurants, cafés, and art galleries within a converted Georgian town house. The Design Centre stocks clothing by more than 20 Irish fashion designers.

➕ J9 ✉ Clarendon Street
🚇 Pearse 🚌 Cross-city buses

## ST STEPHEN'S GREEN CENTRE

A light, airy complex over three floors with good parking. The centre combines more expensive specialist shops with Dunnes department store and bargain emporia, selling everything from fashion and footwear to food and gift ideas.

➕ J10 ✉ Grafton Street
☎ 478 0888 🚇 Pearse
🚌 Cross-city buses

# Interiors

## CAPSULE

Fascinating selection of modern objects with no practical use that would look great displayed in your home.

✚ K9  ✉ 26 Westbury Mall
☎ 672 5379  🚇 Pearse
🚌 Cross-city buses

## THE DRAWING ROOM

Ornate mahogany frames, embroidered cushions, and richly decorated lampstands made from Chinese procelain. Tasteful and expensive.

✚ J9  ✉ 29 Westbury Mall
☎ 677 2083  🚇 Pearse
🚌 Cross-city buses

## FOKO

Stylish contemporary furnishing and gadgets for every room in the house.

✚ J9  ✉ 66–67 South Great George's Street  ☎ 475 5344
🚇 Pearse  🚌 Cross-city buses

## GREEN BUILDING

Haus, one of Dublin's leading contemporary homeware stores. Owned by furniture enthusiast Garett O'Hagan, this is where Dublin style gurus pick up designer items and accessories. The premises are entirely eco-friendly, with solar and wind-generated electricity, waste recycling, and other green features.

✉ Haus, 3–4 Crow Street
☎ 679 5155  🚇 Tara
🚌 Cross-city buses

## KNOBS AND KNOCKERS

Everything you could think of to furnish your door. The Irish Claddagh knocker, based on the symbolic "friendship, loyalty, and love" Claddagh ring, is popular.

✚ K9  ✉ 19 Nassau Street
☎ 671 0288  🚇 Pearse
🚌 Cross-city buses

## L M RUBAN

Amazing selection of ribbons, cords, braids, fringing, and tassels in a myriad widths and a rainbow of hues.

✚ J9  ✉ 19 Westbury Mall
☎ 677 0791  🚇 Pearse
🚌 Cross-city buses

## OBJECTHAUS

A hardware store for the 21st century. Creatively designed everyday objects from cups and saucers to chairs and lamps.

✚ J9  ✉ 16 South Great George's Street  ☎ 677 6442
🚇 Pearse  🚌 Cross-city buses

## STOCK

Furniture, fabrics, rugs, lighting, and an impressive range of kitchen utensils and cookware. Serious cooks will come across more unusual items that are hard to find elsewhere.

✚ J9  ✉ 33–34 South King Street  ☎ 679 4316  🚇 Pearse
🚌 Cross-city buses

## WHICHCRAFT

From decorative divas and handmade lamps to the most stunning mosaic mirrors, Whichcraft's team of Ireland's leading artists and craftworkers reach new heights of innovation. Much of the work is exclusive to the Gallery and includes one-off and limited edition pieces.

✚ H8  ✉ Cow's Lane, Temple Bar  ☎ 474 1011  🚇 Tara Street  🚌 Cross-city buses

## WHAT'S YOUR STYLE?

There are some great shops in Dublin displaying a wide range of home interior products, many produced by Irish craftspeople and also by fashion designers turning their skills to objects and furniture. Interior design is popular worldwide, and Dublin is gaining more shops for the enthusiast. Beautiful items in stone, wood, glass, and other natural materials can be bought in both traditional and contemporary styles. The Georgian architecture of Dublin has influenced designs, with more elaborate Victorian style and cottage chintz favourite alternatives. The contemporary furniture and items influenced by Terence Conran and John Rocha, with pure and simple lines, are becoming increasingly popular.

# Men & Women's Clothing

## IRELAND'S INTERNATIONAL DESIGNERS

Dublin fashion stores carry a great mix of contemporary, alternative, and classic collections. Irish designers to look for include John Rocha, Paul Costelloe, Lainey Keogh, Daryl Kerrigan, and Philip Treacy. Check out the handbags by Helen Cody and Orla Kiely, Vivienne Walsh's intricate jewellery, Pauric Sweeney's witty postmodern accessories (stocked at Hobo, ► right), and Slim Barrett's fairy-tale tiaras.

### ALIAS TOM

One of Dublin's longest-standing men's stores. High fashion on the ground floor and a great selection of suits below: Paul Smith, Versace, Issay Miyake, Donna Karan, Calvin Klein, Hugo Boss, Yves St. Laurent, and many, many more.

➕ K9 ✉ Duke Lane ☎ 671 5443 🚇 Pearse 🚌 Cross-city buses

### AWEAR

Fashionable clothes for young women, with reassuring price tags, Ireland's own high street chain store offers plenty by way of choice. Stock changes every two weeks.

➕ K9 ✉ Grafton Street and other branches ☎ 671 7200 🚇 Pearse 🚌 Cross-city buses

### BT2

Brown Thomas' trendy younger sibling sells more casual clothes like DKNY, French Connection, and Full Circle. Wonderful views of Grafton Street.

➕ K9 ✉ Grafton Street ☎ 605 6666, ext. 1200 🚇 Pearse 🚌 Cross-city buses

### DESIGN CENTRE, POWERSCOURT TOWNHOUSE CENTRE (► 72)

### HOBO

Flagship store of Ireland's most credible and successful street-wear shops. Own-label fleeces, sweats, cords, and combats for men, women, and teenagers. There is another branch on Exchequer Street.

➕ J9 ✉ 6–9 Trinity Street ☎ 670 4869 🚌 Cross-city buses

### LOUIS COPELAND

Acquiring a Louis Copeland suit, made-to-measure or off the peg, is a rite of passage for well-dressed Irish men. The tailor of choice for politicians and society figures.

➕ L10 ✉ 30 Lower Pembroke Street ☎ 661 0110 🚌 10

### LOUISE KENNEDY

The understated elegance of Ireland's leading designer appeals to those with taste. The restored Georgian residence is stylish and calm, and exudes confidence, just like Kennedy's clothing and crystal collections that are sold alongside luxury branded accessories, gift items, and homeware.

➕ M10 ✉ 56 Merrion Square ☎ 662 0056 🚇 Pearse 🚌 Cross-city buses

### SUSAN HUNTER

Tiny but exclusive lingerie store. Ireland's only source of La Perla and Tuttabankem. Pricey but irresistible.

➕ K9 ✉ 13 Westbury Mall ☎ 679 1271 🚇 Pearse 🚌 Cross-city buses

### TRIBE

A favourite shop for Ireland's urban skaters and surfers, Karl Swan's laid-back store is crammed with well-chosen casual clothes, shoes, and accessories.

➕ J10 ✉ First floor, St. Stephen's Green Centre ☎ 475 0311 🚇 Pearse 🚌 Cross-city buses

# Secondhand & Bargains

## CHINA SHOWROOMS

Old-fashioned shop with numerous displays of well-known names in china and crystal glassware where you can always find a bargain.

✚ K7 ✉ 32 Lower Abbey Street ☎ 878 6211 🚇 Tara Street 🚌 Cross-city buses

## EAGER BEAVER

Next-to-new clothing for ladies and gents with several well-known brand names at good prices.

✚ J8 ✉ Crown Alley, Temple Bar ☎ 677 3342 🚇 Tara Street 🚌 Cross-city buses

## FLIP

One of the first ports of call for trendy Irish shoppers on the trail of secondhand jeans, checked shirts, baseball jackets, bowling bags, and other bits of Americana.

✚ J8 ✉ 3–4 Upper Fownes Street, Temple Bar ☎ 671 4299 🚇 Tara Street 🚌 Cross-city buses

## GEORGE STREET MARKET ARCADE

Covered arcade with everything from secondhand records and books to collectables, olives (➤ 79), and a fortune teller.

✚ J9 ✉ Between South Great George's Street and Drury Street 🚇 Pearse 🚌 Cross-city buses

## HARLEQUIN

Classy vintage clothing and accessories, in particular vintage handbags, are a speciality.

✚ J9 ✉ 13 Castle Market ☎ 671 0202 🚇 Pearse 🚌 Cross-city buses

## JENNY VANDER

The place for intricate evening wear, coats, dresses, and separates in delicate and luxurious fabrics as well as shoes, handbags, and jewellery from another era. It's all more antique than secondhand.

✚ J9 ✉ 20 George's Street Arcade, South Great George's Street ☎ 677 0406 🚌 Cross-city buses

## RUFUS THE CAT

The hippest in vintage accessories and men's suits from the 1950s to 1970s, plus some fantastic accessories—early digital watches a speciality. In the same building as Jenny Vander.

✚ J9 ✉ 20 George's Street Arcade, South Great George's Street ☎ 677 0406 🚌 Cross-city buses

## STOCK EXCHANGE

A swap shop where designer labels abound in all shapes, sizes, and styles. Stock is gathered from private clients and often from stores and boutiques. Trust to luck.

✚ Off map ✉ Dundrum Shopping Centre, Dublin 14 ☎ 668 8010 🚌 10

## WILD CHILD

Kitschy, quirky vintage clothing, cards, buttons, accessories, and cosmetics. Everything for anyone impersonating Elvis or the Pink Ladies, immortalized in the hit musical *Grease*.

✚ J9 ✉ 61 and 77 South Great George's Street ☎ 475 5099 🚌 Cross-city buses

## BURIED TREASURE

Although Dubliners tend to be hoarders by nature, the city has always had a great choice of antique, vintage, and secondhand clothing stores. If you are lucky, you can uncover genuine treasures for just a few pounds in these shops and at market stalls. In fact, some items may have been rented or loaned out to wardrobe departments on film sets, so you could be buying a celebrity cast-off.

# Antiques & Art

## CRAFTSMANSHIP

Dublin's rich reputation as a centre of creative excellence dates back several centuries. Irish furniture and silver of the Georgian period embodies some of the finest craftmanship of the late 18th and early 19th centuries (the harp in the hallmark indicates a piece was made in Ireland) and early 20th-century Irish art has attracted worldwide acclaim. Antiques fairs take place regularly in Dublin; the most prestigious events are held two to three times a year at the Royal Dublin Society. For news of auctions around the city, check the daily newspapers.

## APOLLO GALLERY

The specialists in Irish art. Patrons include movie star Sylvester Stallone, Formula One racing team owner Eddie Jordan, Microsoft USA, and Sky TV.

✚ K9 ✉ 51c Dawson Street ☎ 671 2609 🚇 Pearse 🚌 Cross-city buses

## IB JORGENSEN FINE ART

Ireland's favourite fashion designer turned to fine art in 1992 and hasn't looked back. Prepare to pay top prices for works by Jack Yeats, Walter Frederick Osborne, and Mary Swanzy. Solo exhibitions of international contemporary artists are held here.

✚ K9 ✉ 29 Molesworth Street ☎ 661 9758 🚇 Pearse 🚌 Cross-city buses

## JOHN FARRINGTON ANTIQUES

This small shop is packed to the gills with Irish furniture, silver, glass, and *objets d'art*. The precious antique jewellery is especially coveted. Clients include film stars, rock musicians, and super-models.

✚ J9 ✉ 32 Drury Street ☎ 679 1899 🚇 Pearse 🚌 Cross-city buses

## KERLIN GALLERY

This is arguably Dublin's leading contemporary art gallery, established in 1988, showcasing the work of top artists like Dorothy Cross, Feilim Egan, David Godbold, and Paul Seawright. National and international exhibitions are staged monthly.

✚ K9 ✉ Anne's Lane, off South Anne's Street ☎ 670 9093 🚇 Pearse 🚌 Cross-city buses

## LEMON STREET GALLERY

As refreshing to the Irish arts scene as the name would suggest, this gallery offers an intimidation-free zone to those wishing to look at framed and unframed work by a wide range of Irish and international artists. Monthly viewings ensure a steady flow of new work.

✚ K9 ✉ Lemon Street, off Grafton Street ☎ 671 0244 🚇 Pearse 🚌 Cross-city buses

## O'SULLIVAN ANTIQUES

A seasoned expert on the Irish antiques scene, Chantal O'Sullivan's has a keen eye for exquisite items from years gone by. You'll find everything here from mahogany furniture and gilt mirrors to marble mantelpieces, garden statues, and delicate glass.

✚ G9 ✉ 43–44 Francis Street ☎ 454 1143 🚌 78A, 123

## SILVER SHOP

Wide range of antique silver and silver-plate from the conventional to the unusual Irish portrait miniatures. Prices start low and head up into the thousands. It's a great place for imaginative gifts.

✚ J9 ✉ First Floor, Powerscourt Townhouse Centre, Clarendon Street ☎ 679 4147 🚇 Pearse 🚌 Cross-city buses

# Books & Music

### CATHACH BOOKS

Dublin's leading rare and antiquarian bookshop, specializing in books of Irish interest with a particular emphasis on 20th-century literature.

✚ K9 ✉ 10 Duke Street ☎ 671 8676 🚊 Pearse 🚌 Cross-city buses

### CELTIC NOTE

One of the country's best specialist Irish music stores has everything from classical to traditional, rock to contemporary.

✚ K9 ✉ Nassau Street ☎ 670 4157 🚊 Pearse 🚌 Cross-city buses

### CHAPTERS

Large shop piled high with books on all kinds of interesting subjects, including Celtic calligraphy, and lots on Dublin itself. Watch out for the special offers.

✚ J9 ✉ 1089 Abbey St. Middle ☎ 872 3279 🚊 Tara Street 🚌 Cross-city buses

### CHARLES BYRNE

Established in 1870, Charles Byrne are renowned for their expertise in stringed instruments and stock Ireland's best range of *bodhráns*, handmade by experts.

✚ J9 ✉ 21–22 Lower Stephen Street ☎ 478 1773 🚊 Pearse 🚌 Cross-city buses

### CLADDAGH RECORDS

Specialist music shop—folk, traditional, and ethnic music.

✚ J8 ✉ 2 Cecilia Street, Temple Lane ☎ 677 0262 🚊 Tara Street 🚌 Cross-city buses

### HODGES & FIGGIS

Well-known bookstore with a large selection and excellent ordering facilities. Coffee shop on the first floor.

✚ K9 ✉ 56–58 Dawson Street ☎ 677 4754 🚊 Pearse 🚌 Cross-city buses

### J. MCNEILS

Trading for more than 150 years, McNeil's is a delightful shop that offers excellent advice on its large selection of Irish instruments and has skilled craftsmen to carry out repairs.

✚ H8 ✉ 140 Capel Street ☎ 872 2159 🚊 Tara Street 🚌 Cross-city buses

### MCCULLOUGH PIGOTT'S

Highly respected by music lovers who while away an hour or so gazing at the musical instruments and browsing through the sheet music.

✚ K9 ✉ 25 Suffolk Street ☎ 677 3188 🚊 Pearse 🚌 Cross-city buses

### WALTONS

Irish music specialists for more than 75 years. Harps, *bodhráns*, whistles, pipes, flutes, banjos, mandolins, bouzoukis, accordions, and much more. Also at North Frederick Street.

✚ J9 ✉ 69–70 South Great George's Street ☎ 475 0661 🚊 Pearse 🚌 Cross-city buses

### WINDING STAIR

Quaint bookshope with bargains and a café (► 71) overlooking the river

✚ J8 ✉ 40 Lower Ormond Quay ☎ 873 3292 🚊 Tara Street 🚌 Cross-city buses

### TRADITION LIVES ON

Irish traditional music is played in pubs all over the city every night of the week and is generally free. Music is often spontaneous, with musicians joining in an impromptu *seisún* (session). The Irish have grown up with this music; it has been handed down through the generations and instruments are learned instinctively by watching others. The basic instruments of the session are the *bodhrán*, or frame drum (► 18) and the fiddle, together with flutes or whistles. The accordion, musical spoons, guitars, banjos, and *uillean* pipes all add their extra, individual sound. All these instruments and sheet music can be found in the excellent traditional music shops in the city, together with CDs you will not find outside Ireland. The music can also have a contemporary approach, inspired by the likes of Altan, who mix rock and folk, as well as others who have introduced rap or African influences into the traditional sound.

# Irish Crafts

## MADE IN IRELAND

If you're looking for something of modern Ireland for your home, check out the following stores favoured by Irish people as well as visitors:

• Jerpoint glass jugs, glasses, bowls, and candlesticks are heavy, hand-blown pieces of simple design with occasional colour bursts.

• Irish fashion designer John Rocha has brought Waterford crystal up to date and back into fashion with a designer line that is minimalist and popular with younger buyers. His glasses, bowls, vases, and platters come in three styles.

• Nicholas Mosse's sponged pottery is so popular that Tiffany & Co has commissioned a pattern. His colourful table settings, jugs, bowls, and kitchenware are a delight.

• Louis Mulcahy is one of Ireland's most prolific ceramicists, and this spacious store is a perfect showcase for his extensive range of pottery items. Packaging and shipping is easily arranged by helpful staff.

## BLARNEY WOOLLEN MILLS

A classic shop with an amazing collection of sweaters, woollen rugs, and throws, Irish tweeds and linen, alongside great names like Waterford Crystal, Belleek, Royal Tara, Irish Dresden.

✉ K9  ✉ 21–23 Nassau Street
☎ 671 0068  🚏 Pearse
🚌 Cross-city buses

## CLEO

If handknit sweaters, tweedy skirts, and high-end country style is your style, Cleo's is the place for you. A company run by three generations of the Joyce family since 1936, Cleo's specialize in clothes made in knitters' and weavers' homes from natural fibres of Irish origin. Many of the designs are drawn from Ireland's past. Very expensive

✚ K10  ✉ 18 Kildare Street
☎ 676 1421  🚏 Pearse
🚌 Cross-city buses

## CRAFTS CENTRE OF IRELAND

Good selection of Irish crafts not readily available in other stores—whimsical rugs, watercolours, mirrors, candlesticks, a variety of pottery, glass, and ironwork.

✚ J10  ✉ Top floor, St. Stephen's Green Centre
☎ 475 4526  🚏 Pearse
🚌 Cross-city buses

## DESIGNYARD

A centre for crafts and decorative arts. The second floor has ceramics, textiles, and interior design. Note how the floor mosaic traces the path of an underground river, and the wrought-iron gates imitate a Dublin street map. The stunning downstairs jewellery gallery showcases Irish designers.

✉ K9  ✉ 12 East Essex Street
☎ 677 8453  🚏 Tara Street
🚌 Cross-city buses

## HOUSE OF IRELAND

Traditional Irish fashion, crafts, Waterford crystal, china, and Aran knitwear.

✚ K9  ✉ 38 Nassau Street
☎ 671 6133  🚏 Pearse
🚌 Cross-city buses

## KILKENNY DESIGN CENTRE

An essential stopping point for stylish Irish decorative objects for the home, glass, books, fashion, and jewellery.

✚ K9  ✉ Nassau Street
☎ 677 7066  🚏 Pearse
🚌 Cross-city buses

## TEMPLE BAR POTTERY & CRAFT SHOP

Fine bone china made on the premises and each piece hand painted in the ceramic studio.

✚ J8  ✉ 45 Temple Bar
☎ 679 4016  🚏 Tara Street
🚌 Cross-city buses

## TRINITY CRAFT CENTRE

Inspiring potters, jewellers, and textile designers work and sell in around 35 small workshops here. Look for pieces by quirky silversmith Alan Ardiff and scarves by Mel Bradly (who also works for John Rocha and Louise Kennedy).

✉ L9  ✉ Pearse Street
☎ 677 5655  🚏 Pearse
🚌 13

# Food & Wine

**BIG CHEESE COMPANY**
In addition to a huge variety of cheeses from worldwide sources, this shop stocks other foods imported from France, Italy, and Belgium. Buy excellent American groceries or superb Dutch cheeses. The only shop in Dublin to stock Jewish kosher foods.
➕ J9 ✉ 14/15 Trinity Street ☎ 671 1399 🚉 Pearse 🚌 Cross-city buses

**DOUGLAS FOOD COMPANY**
Epicurean haven for those in a hurry, with the best caviar, *foie gras*, pastries, wines, and French cheese.
➕ J8 ✉ 53 Main Street, Donnybrook ☎ 269 4066 🚌 10, 46a

**THE EPICUREAN FOOD HALL**
Home-made ice cream, sweet pastries, bagels, vegetarian, and organic sellers contend with each other for the most divine smells each day.
➕ J9 ✉ Upper Liffey Street 🚉 Tara Street 🚌 Cross-city buses

**HOUSE OF LIME AND LEMONGRASS**
Additive-free pasta sauces, chutneys, mustards, bottled olives, roast garlic, and sun-dried tomatoes.
➕ K8 ✉ 2–3 Mary's Abbey, Capel Street ☎ 872 2965 🚌 Cross-city buses

**LE MAISON DES GOURMANDS**
A mouth-watering array of patisserie sit in the window of this eponymous food hall; inside are savoury treats and the finest French packaged goods.
➕ K10 ✉ 115 Castle Market ☎ 672 7258 🚉 Pearse 🚌 Cross-city buses

**MAGILLS**
Salami, meats, bread, cheese, coffee, herbs, spices, and every sort of packaged delicacy you can imagine.
➕ J9 ✉ 14 Clarendon Street ☎ 671 3830 🚉 Pearse 🚌 Cross-city buses

**MITCHELL & SON WINE MERCHANTS**
The ground floor houses Dublin's oldest and possibly finest wine merchants stocking interesting and exclusive vintages in the basement.
➕ K10 ✉ 21 Kildare Street ☎ 676 0766 🚉 Pearse 🚌 Cross-city buses

**THE OLIVE MAN**
Over 25 different sorts of olives, plus sun-dried and spiced vegetables. Divinely scented handmade soaps.
➕ J9 ✉ George's Street Market Arcade, South Great George's Street 🚌 Cross-city buses

**SHERIDANS CHEESE SHOP**
This glorious shop packed with massive blocks of cheese is a wonderful showcase for the Irish farmhouse varieties that are winning awards worldwide. Also sells other excellent Irish foods including salmon and jams.
➕ K9 ✉ 11 South Anne's Street ☎ 679 3143 🚉 Pearse 🚌 Cross-city buses

**SATURDAY MARKET**
Irish food lovers spend their Saturdays in Meeting House Square at Temple Bar, where the weekly food market sells a variety of produce ranging from Japanese sushi to Mexican burritos. Local Irish produce includes fresh breads, jams, yoghurts, and vegetables. Those with a sweeter tooth will enjoy the handmade fudge and chocolate stalls or freshly cooked waffles and crêpes. Among the other stalls at this gastronomic paradise are cheeses, seasonal fruits, home-made quiches, olives, and Spanish tapas. Or you can take a seat to sample fresh oysters seasoned with lemon juice, Tabasco, and black pepper. It poses just one dilemma—can you resist tucking into your purchases before the next meal?

# Theatre

## FESTIVAL

You would expect the capital of literary Ireland to be overflowing with theatrical talent—and you would be right. *Riverdance* and *Dancing at Lughnasa* both played to Irish audiences before receiving global acclaim, and Martin McDonaugh packed Dubliners in to see his *Lenane* trilogy prior to winning several Tony awards on Broadway. In contrast, the annual Christmas pantomimes see Irish celebrities ham up traditional fairy tales, usually with elaborate story embellishment and even more extravagant costumes. The Dublin Theater Festival and fringe continues to grow in breadth, stature, and popularity each year. Events are staged throughout October in traditional and less conventional locations around the city, and tickets are usually available at short notice.

## ABBEY

The national theatre played a vital role in the renaissance of Irish culture at the end of the 19th century. The quality of playwriting and performances is rarely surpassed. Many first runs go to New York's Broadway or London's West End.
➕ K7 ✉ 26 Lower Abbey Street ☎ 878 7222
🚈 Connelly/Tara Street
🚌 Cross-city buses

## ANDREW'S LANE

The main stage and a smaller studio upstairs attract a steady stream of young theatre-goers.
➕ K9 ✉ 9–17 Andrew's Lane ☎ 679 5720 🚈 Pearse
🚌 Cross-city buses

## CRYPT ARTS CENTRE

An elegant but intimate setting in Dublin Castle's church crypt. Used by many of Dublin's younger companies for experimental productions.
➕ h8 ✉ Dublin Castle, Dame Street ☎ 671 3387 🚈 Tara Street 🚌 Cross-city buses

## FOCUS THEATRE

This tiny space has seen many surprises and excellent perform-ances. Movie star Gabriel Byrne was once a regular.
➕ L11 ✉ 6 Pembroke Place, off Pembroke Street ☎ 676 3071 🚌 10

## GAIETY

An integral part of Dublin theatreland, with a varied programme of pantomime, opera, musicals, comedies, classic plays, and touring shows. After the curtain goes down on Friday and Saturday, the theatre transforms into a salsa and soul nightclub.
➕ j9 ✉ South King Street ☎ 677 1717 🚈 Pearse
🚌 Cross-city buses

## GATE

Some of Dublin's most inspired and sophisticated theatre, performed in an 18th-century building. Many Dublin thespians and critics rate the works performed here as the best in Ireland.
➕ J6 ✉ Parnell Square ☎ 874 4045 🚌 Cross-city buses

## OLYMPIA

Dublin's oldest theatre mounts mainstream shows including musicals, stand-up comedy, and traditional Christmas pantomimes.
➕ g7 ✉ 72 Dame Street ☎ 677 7744 🚌 Cross-city buses

## PEACOCK

The Abbey's younger sibling in the same complex is a platform for emerging Irish talent.
➕ K7 ✉ 26 Lower Abbey Street ☎ 878 7222
🚈 Connelly/Tara Street
🚌 Cross-city buses

## PROJECT ARTS CENTRE

Young theatre groups stage new and experimental performances at lunchtime, in the evening, and late at night.
➕ g7 ✉ 39 East Essex Street, ☎ 679 6622 🚈 Tara Street
🚌 Cross-city buses

# Movies

### BLANCHARDSTOWN UCI

A nine-screen multiplex outside the city with a comprehensive choice and good facilities. Films tend to run longer here than at the more central cinemas.

✚ Off map ✉ Blanchardstown Shopping Centre ☎ 1850 52 53 54 🚊 Suburban line Connolly to Blanchardstown 🚌 38, 38A, 39, 39X, 70, 70X, 236

### CLASSIC

Old-fashioned movie theatre with weekly Friday-night interactive screening of *The Rocky Horror Show*.

✚ Off map ✉ Harolds Cross ☎ 492 3699 🚌 54A

### IRISH FILM CENTRE

Members and guests can view art films or limited release movies on the two screens in this interesting conversion of old houses. Restaurant, bar, shop, and movie archive. Membership can be arranged on the spot.

✚ h7 ✉ 6 Eustace Street, Temple Bar ☎ 679 5744 🚊 Tara Street 🚌 Cross-city buses

### ORMONDE

The only movie theatre worth visting on Dublin's south side. Five screens show a mixture of new releases and children's movies.

✚ Off map ✉ Lower Kilmacud Road, Stillorgan ☎ 278 0000 🚌 46A

### PARNELL CENTRE

The centre houses a nine-screen UCG multiplex. Entertainment includes simulated rides, computer games, well-supervised amusements, themed bars and restaurants, fast food outlets, virtual reality experiences, and a parking area. You could spend hours here without catching a glimpse of daylight. Shooters bar is popular with the young.

✚ H7 ✉ Parnell Street ☎ 872 8444; 872 8400 🚌 Cross-city buses

### SAVOY

This old-style movie theatre hosts most Irish movie premieres and their parties. Modern concessions include five wide screens, drink holder, and Dolby sound systems.

✚ K9 ✉ O'Connell Street ☎ 874 6000 🚌 Cross-city buses

### SCREEN

Fringe and mainstream movies on three screens. Good discounts on matinees. Bring your own munchies—the selection here leaves much to be desired.

✚ k6 ✉ D'Olier Street ☎ 672 5500 🚊 Pearse 🚌 Cross-city buses

### STER CENTURY

Ireland's biggest and newest multiplex has 14 screens including The Big Fella, Europe's largest. Seats look and feel like sports cars, sound and picture quality are state of the art, as are the snacks and café facilities.

✚ Off map to northwest ✉ Liffey Valley Centre, Fonthill Road ☎ 605 5700 🚌 78A

### DID YOU KNOW?

• James Joyce was a manager at one of Ireland's earliest movie theatres, the Volta, which opened in 1909.
• Dublin has one of the highest per capita movie attendances in Europe.
• The Irish Film Centre, the Savoy, and the Screen are all venues for the Dublin film festival in March.
• Seats are cheaper during the day.
• There is a no-smoking policy in all movie theatres.
• New films are sometimes released earlier in Ireland than in the UK due to the film distribution system.

# Live Music Venues

## THE CLASSICS

Dublin has a thriving classical music and opera scene, though performances are irregular. The National Concert Hall stages a full programme but other venues offer seasonal performances only. To find out about forthcoming events, call the box offices direct or check the listings in the *Irish Times*. Reservations are recommended for most performances.

## STAR TURN

There's no shortage of big international names appearing in Dublin. When it comes to the live music scene, the city's major concert venues such as Lansdowne Road, the Point Theatre, and the Ambassador have featured major stars, including Robbie Williams, Neil Diamond, Rod Stewart, and Westlife, on their programmes. Throughout the city the well known and not so well known can be found in a host of smaller venues. For the big names you will have to book well in advance; for those appearing in the clubs check out the free events papers or ask at the tourist information office.

## AMBASSADOR

Small live music venue. Visiting acts include international big names.
➕ J6 ✉ Parnell Square
☎ 648 6060 🚇 Connolly
🚌 Cross-city buses

## BANK OF IRELAND ARTS CENTRE

Classical recitals by amateur and professional groups from Ireland and overseas.
➕ j7 ✉ 2 Foster Place
☎ 671 1488 🚇 Tara Street
🚌 Cross-city buses

## GAIETY THEATRE

The Gaiety Theatre (► 80) plays host to Dublin's most professional and prolific opera society. The twice-yearly programmes (usually held in spring and autumn) include much-loved favourites as well as more obscure works.
☎ 453 5519

## HUGH LANE MUNICIPAL GALLERY OF MODERN ART

Classical recitals are held at noon every Sunday in this impressive art gallery. The programme runs year-round with a break in summer. Free admission.
➕ J6 ✉ Parnell Square North
☎ 874 1903 🚇 Connolly
🚌 Cross-city buses

## JOHNNY FOXES

People come from near and far for the turf fires, live traditional music, *céilí* dancing, and delicious seafood. If you want to eat, be sure to reserve ahead.
➕ Off map to southwest
✉ Dublin Mountains, Glencullen, County Dublin ☎ 295 5647
🚌 44B

## NATIONAL CONCERT HALL

Busy Georgian concert hall with a modern auditorium and superb world-class acoustics. Top artists perform here when they are in town. The John Field Room, the National Concert Hall's annexe space, hosts performances of chamber music among its varied programme of modern and classical music. It has a seating capacity of 250.
➕ K11 ✉ Earlsfort Terrace
☎ 475 1572

## OLYMPIA

Midnight concerts in Dublin's oldest theatre are massively popular on the live circuit.
➕ h7 ✉ 74 Dame Street
☎ 677 7744 🚌 Cross-city buses

## TEMPLE BAR MUSIC CENTRE

A premier music venue that also stages fashion shows, club nights, and dance events. Café, bar, and good live music. Upstairs balcony.
➕ h7 ✉ Curved Street
☎ 670 9202 🚇 Tara Street
🚌 Cross-city buses

## WHELAN'S

A well-run venue with good acoustics, plenty of space, and a great atmosphere. Up-and-coming Irish groups and overseas bands on tour often headline.
➕ J10 ✉ 25 Wexford Street
☎ 478 0766 🚌 14, 14A, 47, 47A, 47B, 83

# Pubs & Bars

### BRAZEN HEAD

Reputedly the oldest bar in town (trading for more than 800 years), the Brazen Head has an old-world charm. The walls are covered with memorabilia from the pub's past. The Brazen Head has a reputation for good food, drink, and Irish music sessions.

✚ G8 ✉ 20 Bridge Street Lower ☎ 679 5186 🚌 21, 21A

### BUSKERS

One of Dublin's liveliest theme bars with its Dublin streetscape, traditional Irish Whiskey corner, and cosmopolitan atmosphere attracting the city's young set.

✚ j6 ✉ Temple Bar Hotel, Fleet Street ☎ 677 3333 🚊 Tara Street 🚌 Cross-city buses

### CAFÉ EN SEINE

The beautiful interior of this exceedingly long bar has strikingly high ceilings supporting French bistro lighting. The relaxed daytime atmosphere hots up in the evening when the bar fills out with office workers.

✚ d/e5 ✉ 40 Dawson Street ☎ 677 4369 🚊 Pearse 🚌 Cross-city buses

### THE CHOCOLATE BAR

Hot and cold designer sandwiches by day for trendies and office workers; a popular haunt by night. Great cocktails.

✚ K10 ✉ Old Harcourt Street Station, Upper Hatch Street ☎ 478 0166 🕐 Food served at lunchtime only 🚌 Cross-city buses

### HOGAN'S

A fashionable bar packed with Dublin's beautiful young things on their way to nearby dance clubs.

✚ h9 ✉ 35 South Great George's Street ☎ 677 5904 🚌 Cross-city buses

### THE LONG HALL

Time seems to have stood still in this traditional hostelry, with a long bar, smoked glass, and detailed paintwork.

✚ h9 ✉ 51 South Great George's Street ☎ 475 1590 🚌 Cross-city buses

### MESSRS MAGUIRE

If you fancy a change from Guinness try the excellent beers brewed in the basement at this popular labyrinth of bars and cosy snugs. Frequent live music and good food.

✚ k6 ✉ 1–2 Burgh Quay ☎ 670 5777 🚊 Tara Street 🚌 Cross-city buses

### O'NEILLS

O'Neills always offers a friendly welcome. It is renowned for its ageless character and numerous alcoves and snugs. Good food, particularly the lunchtime carvery.

✚ j7/8 ✉ 2 Suffolk Street ☎ 679 3656 🚊 Pearse 🚌 Cross-city buses

### STAG'S HEAD

Built in 1770 and remodelled in 1895, this pub has retained wonderful stained-glass windows, wood carvings, and iron work. Off a cobblestoned lane.

✚ h8 ✉ 1 Dame Court ☎ 679 3701 🚌 Cross-city buses

### EVEN MORE PUBS

There are so many good pubs in Dublin well worth a visit. It's just a case of trying several and you'll soon find your favourites. Below are a few more:

**McDaids** (3 Harry Street)—this dark high-ceilinged pub is well known for its literary connections.

**Davy Byrnes** (21 Duke Street)—for James Joyce fans but now more cocktails than pints.

**The Old Stand** (37 Exchequer Street)—popular among sport enthusiasts as sports *craic* and rugby chat abounds.

**Ryan's** (28 Parkgate Street)—with its fabulous Victorian decor, this pub has been in the Ryan family since 1920.

**Porterhouse Brewery Company** (16–18 Parliament Street)—microbrewery and pub with pleasant interior.

**Doheny & Nesbitt** (5 Lower Baggot Street)—glorious old pub, renowned for 130 years. Lively *craic*.

**Mother Redcaps** (40–48 Back Lane)—huge atmospheric pub with some great music sessions.

**Mulligans** (8 Poolbeg Street)—most celebrated for its legendary perfectly poured pint of Guinness. Great 19th-century surroundings, too.

### CHEERS!

When toasting each other, Irish people say "sláinte!" (pronounced slawn-cha) meaning "health!" It gets easier to say as the night progresses.

# Dance Clubs

## DANCE

When looking for the best dance clubs in Dublin, go by the name of that particular night at the club rather than the name of the venue itself. Most good dance nights are independently run gigs organized by promoters and staged in different places around town. *The Event Guide*, distributed free in bars and cafés around the city, has the most comprehensive and accurate listings.

## GAY SCENE

HAM at The PoD every Friday is Dublin's most happening gay clubnight. For pre-club drinks and dance nights try The George on South Great George's Street (Sunday Bingo is especially popular). Don't miss the Alternative Miss Ireland (an outrageous drag beauty pageant) if you are in town on St. Patrick's Festival—around March 17.

## CLUB ANNABEL'S

One of Dublin's largest and most successful clubs. Frequented by young professionals.

✚ Off map ✉ Burlington Hotel, Upper Leeson Street ☎ 660 5222 🚌 13, 46A

## CLUB M

A lively club in the heart of Temple Bar. Mainly aimed at the full-on cruising crowd who boogie into the early hours to mainstream chart hits. Inspirational light system.

✚ j7 ✉ Blooms Hotel, 6 Anglesea Street, Temple Bar ☎ 671 5622 🚉 Tara Street 🚌 Cross-city buses

## FITZSIMONS

The city's most vibrant and happening nightspot. The Ballroom nightclub has regular theme nights and changing DJs play a mix of pop, dance, and chart hits. Traditional Irish music and dance takes place nightly on the ground floor and the upper floor has an intimate riverside restaurant.

✚ h7 ✉ 21–22 Wellington Quay, Temple Bar ☎ 677 9315 🚉 Tara Street 🚌 Cross-city buses

## THE KITCHEN

Ultra-hip dance club in the basement of U2's cosmopolitan Clarence Hotel. The style of the music and clubbers varies dramatically from night to night, so check the local press for details of what's on.

✚ g7 ✉ Clarence Hotel, 6–8 Wellington Quay ☎ 677 6635 🚉 Tara Street 🚌 Cross-city buses

## LILLIE'S BORDELLO

A home-away-from-home for pop and movie stars. House, chart, and oldie music.

✚ j/k8 ✉ Adam Court, Grafton Street ☎ 679 9204 🚉 Pearse 🚌 Cross-city buses

## THE PALACE

Dublin's first super-club that fits hoards of happy young dancers. Music is a mainstream mish-mash of popular chart tunes.

✚ J11 ✉ Camden Street ☎ 478 0808 🚉 Pearse 🚌 Cross-city buses

## POD

The Place of Dance is one of the hippest clubs in town. Tight door policy restricts entry to the stylish and sober. Different club each evening but a good mix of happy house and dance floor favourites.

✚ J11 ✉ 35 Harcourt Street ☎ 478 0166 🚌 Cross-city buses

## RENARDS

Late-night club with busy basement dance floor (members only), a ground-floor café/bar, and an upstairs VIP area populated by thirtysomethings from the worlds of fashion, media, and film. Music comes second to the chat.

✚ k9 ✉ 33–35 South Frederick Street ☎ 677 5876 🚉 Pearse 🚌 Cross-city buses

## RÍ RÁ

A good night out. Informal and fashionable with a chill-out area upstairs.

✚ h8 ✉ 1 Exchequer Street ☎ 677 4835 🚉 Tara Street 🚌 Cross-city buses

# Sports

## GAELIC GAMES

Gaelic football and hurling are fast, physical games, and the All-Ireland finals are played before sell-out crowds in early and late September. Hurling is an ancient sport whose roots go back to pre-Christian times, and both games have been actively promoted by the Gaelic Athletic Association since 1884.

➕ L4 ✉ Croke Park Stadium ☎ 836 3222 🚌 3, 11, 16, 51A

## GOLF

The growth of championship golf courses in Dublin is staggering. Many clubs welcome non-members, and fees are reasonable. The most famous are Royal Dublin and Portmarnock; also try Castle, Grange, Woodbrook Malahide, Miltown, Hermitage, and Island. Or try one of the city's pitch-and-putt courses. The Irish Open Golf Championships are staged in July at different courses around the country.

## GREYHOUND RACING

Catch this popular activity Wednesday, Thursday, and Saturday.

➕ P9 ✉ Shelbourne Park Stadium, South Lotts Road ☎ 668 3502 🚌 Lansdowne Road 🚌 3

## HORSE RACING

Leopardstown Race Course is one of Ireland's busiest. Open all year, it hosts the Hennessy Gold Cup and traditional post-Christmas festival, among other events.

➕ Off map to south ✉ Leopardstown Road ☎ 289 3607 🚌 86, 118

## ROLLERBLADING

The smooth, flat, picturesque walk along Sandymount Strand is popular with local in-line skaters who whoosh along the seafront day and night. A stunning location in spring and summer.

➕ Off map ✉ Sandymount Strand, Sandymount 🚌 2, 3

## RUGBY

Ireland's fans remain enthusiastic despite the national team's changing fortunes. Details of fixtures for local clubs, like Bective Rangers, Wesley, and Blackrock, are published in the local press. Better, soak up the atmosphere of a major tournament at Lansdowne Road or in one of the many pubs showing the match on screen.

➕ Q11 ✉ Lansdowne Road Stadium, Ballsbridge ☎ 668 4601 🚌 Lansdowne Road 🚌 5, 7, 7A, 8, 45

## SOCCER

Since the World Cup in 1990, the Irish have become soccer fanatics, and Dublin usually stands still when the national team plays. The season runs from August to May, and you can buy tickets for matches at Tolka Park Stadium (shared home to Shamrock Rovers and Shelbourne Rovers), at the gate.

➕ Off map ✉ Tolka Park Stadium, Griffith Avenue ☎ 837 5536/5754 🚌 11, 11A, 13A, 19A

## THE IRISH GAME

The Gaelic Athletic Association (GAA) is Ireland's largest sporting and cultural organization. Their museum, dedicated to the national games, is housed in the home of Gaelic sport, Croke Park, and is well worth a visit. Interactive, and with plenty to educate and enthuse visitors, the exhibition gives the past, present, and future of popular Irish sport.

**GAA Museum**

➕ L7 ✉ New Stand, Croke Park, Jones Road ☎ 855 8176 🕐 May–Sep: daily 9:30–5; Oct–Apr: Tue–Sat 10–5, Sun 12–5 🚌 3, 11, 16, 51A

## SNOOKER

Jason's Snooker Hall is home to Ken Doherty and a host of rising stars.

✉ 56 Ranelagh ☎ 497 5983 🚌 11, 11A, 13B, 44, 48A, 86

# Luxury Hotels

## PRICES

For a double room per night:
Luxury        over €200
Mid-Range   €85–200
Budget        under €85

Dublin hotel rates historically included bed, full Irish breakfast, service charge, and VAT (currently 21 percent) in the quoted price, but with the arrival of so many new international chains to the capital, it is always wise to check when booking.

## ROOM IN THE CITY

The number of hotel rooms in Dublin has risen dramatically since the mid-1990s. Even with all this extra availability and with the increased popularity of Dublin as a holiday and a business destination, it is always advisable to secure hotel accommodation before arriving in the city.

## BERKELEY COURT

Superlative comfort and tranquillity with chintz sofas, thick carpets, and blissful quiet.
➕ Off map ✉ Lansdowne Road ☎ 660 1711; fax 661 7238 ✉ Lansdowne Road 🚌 5, 7, 7A, 8, 45

## CLARENCE

Chic, modern interior with soft suede upholstery and stunning floral arrangements. Guest rooms are small, apart from the fine duplex penthouse.
➕ b/c2 ✉ 6–8 Wellington Quay ☎ 670 9000; fax 670 7800 🚆 Tara Street 🚌 Cross-city buses

## CLARION STEPHEN'S HALL

Tastefully furnished all-suite hotel. Rooms have state-of-the-art office facilities. Fine restaurant.
➕ K11 ✉ 14–17 Lower Leeson Street ☎ 638 1111; fax 638 1122 🚌 Cross-city buses

## FITZWILLIAM

Stylishly designed by Terence Conran, with a superb restaurant.
➕ d5 ✉ St. Stephen's Green ☎ 478 7000; fax 478 7878 🚆 Pearse 🚌 Cross-city buses

## GRESHAM

Ultimate luxury and attentive service. Huge, elegant bedrooms combine traditional style with modern comfort. Several bars and lounges, the Aberdeen restaurant, and a fitness suite.
➕ K6 ✉ Upper O'Connell Street ☎ 874 6881; fax 878 7175 🚆 Connolly 🚌 Cross-city buses

## HERBERT PARK

Modern, bright, airy hotel in Dublin's exclusive residential area. Quiet comfort with rooms overlooking Herbert Park.
➕ Off P12 ✉ Ballsbridge ☎ 667 2200; fax 667 2595 ✉ Lansdowne Road 🚌 5, 7, 7A, 8, 45

## MERRION

This impressive hotel, originally four Georgian houses, has luxurious bedrooms with good business facilities and spacious bathrooms. Gym, pool, and spa.
➕ L10 ✉ Upper Merrion Street ☎ 603 0600; fax 603 0700 🚆 Pearse 🚌 Cross-city buses

## THE MORRISON

Modern designer heaven, the Morrison is east-meets-west cosmopolitan. Vibrant guests converge on the lobby, bars, and restaurants at all times.
➕ b1 ✉ Lower Ormond Quay ☎ 887 2400; fax 878 3185 🚌 Cross-city buses

## THE SHELBOURNE

This historic hotel is an integral part of Dublin society. Friendly service, a gentle charm, and rooms overlooking the green.
➕ e5 ✉ 27 St. Stephen's Green ☎ 676 6471; fax 661 6006 🚆 Pearse 🚌 Cross-city buses

## WESTBURY

In the heart of Dublin's shopping district. Watch life come and go from the wonderful open foyer.
➕ d4 ✉ Grafton Street ☎ 679 1122; fax 679 7078 🚆 Pearse 🚌 Cross-city buses

# Mid-Range Hotels

### GRAFTON CAPITAL
In the heart of Dublin's shopping and cultural area, with many restaurants, cafés, and attractions just around the corner. Traditional Georgian town house with friendly and helpful staff and modern rooms.

✚ c4  ✉ Lower Stephen's Street  ☎ 648 1100; fax 648 1122  🅿 Pearse  🚌 Cross-city buses

### HARRINGTON HALL
A beautifully restored Georgian guest-house with genteel public areas and generously proportioned guest rooms. An elegant address in the city centre.

✚ J11  ✉ 70 Harcourt Street  ☎ 475 3497; fax 475 4544  🚌 Cross-city buses

### JURYS INN CHRISTCHURCH
Rates are calculated on a per room basis (up to three adults, or two adults with two children). Lovely bar and restaurant plus a parking area.

✚ a3  ✉ Christchurch Place  ☎ 454 0000; fax 454 0012  🚌 Cross-city buses

### MESPIL
Efficient, spacious, and modern; near the Grand Canal and convenient for business travellers.

✚ M11  ✉ Mespil Road  ☎ 667 1222; fax 667 1244  🅿 Grand Canal Dock  🚌 10, 11, 11A, 11B, 13, 46A, 46B

### MOLESWORTH COURT
These pleasantly decorated one- and two-bedroom apartments can be rented for one night or more. Quiet, and near Grafton Street.

✚ k9  ✉ Schoolhouse Lane, off Molesworth Street  ☎ 676 4799; fax 676 4982  🅿 Pearse  🚌 Cross-city buses

### THE MORGAN
This gem of a hotel has Egyptian cotton sheets, spacious bathrooms, and excellent in-room facilities including ISDN lines, VCRs, and compact disc players.

✚ d1/2  ✉ 10 Fleet Street, Temple Bar  ☎ 679 3939; fax 679 3946  🅿 Tara Street  🚌 Cross-city buses

### PEMBROKE TOWNHOUSE
The excellent service in this Georgian-style house has won it a loyal following. Executive boardroom and access to local health club.

✚ Off map  ✉ 90 Pembroke Road  ☎ 660 0277; fax 660 0291  🅿 Lansdowne Road  🚌 5, 7, 7A, 10

### STAUNTON'S ON THE GREEN
Large Georgian guest house with garden and well-equipped rooms. Close to museums, stores, and galleries.

✚ K11  ✉ 83 St. Stephen's Green  ☎ 478 2300; fax 478 2263  🅿 Pearse  🚌 Cross-city buses

### TRINITY LODGE
Elegant Georgian guest house opposite Trinity College. Large, beautifully decorated rooms.

✚ e3  ✉ 12 South Frederick Street  ☎ 679 5044; fax 679 5223  🅿 Pearse  🚌 Cross-city buses

### GOLF HOTELS
Ireland's reputation as a world-class golfing destination is now undisputed and there are some excellent hotels with great courses just outside the city.

**Portmarnock Hotel and Golf Links**
Comfort, good food, and world-class golf. The hotel's 18-hole course was designed by Bernard Langer. Near the airport.

✚ Off map  ✉ Strand Road Portmarnock  ☎ 846 0611; fax 846 2442

**Citywest Hotel Conference, Leisure and Golf Resort**
With two on-site, 18-hole golf courses and a range of leisure facilities, Citywest offers an excellent place to stay only 20 minutes from the city centre.

✚ Off map  ✉ Saggart  ☎ 401 0500; fax 401 8565

**Deer Park Hotel & Golf Courses**
Only 14km (8.5 miles) from the city centre and situated on a quiet hillside overlooking the sea, the Deer Park features Ireland's largest golf complex with five courses including a 6,104m (6,678 yard), par 72, 18-hole course.

✚ Off map  ✉ Howth  ☎ 832 2624; fax 839 2405

# Budget Accommodation

## BUDGET STAY

Budget accommodation comes in three different formats.

**Hotels:** Dublin city centre is well supplied with clean, functional, new hotels that offer somewhere to stay at the right price. Most of the smarter bets are situated around the Temple Bar area and are popular with visiting groups.

**Hostels:** Forget the traditional image, Dublin has a good selection of very low cost hostels that give guests the option of single or double bedrooms as well as the more usual dorms. Many offer good cafés, laundry rooms, and internet access.

**Guest-houses:** There are many reputable bed-and-breakfast establishments working within the auspices of the Irish Tourist Board. Information from the Dublin Tourist Authority ☎ 605 7777

## TRINITY COLLEGE

If you are planning a long stay in the summer, it is possible to rent student rooms in Trinity College (☎ 608 1177; fax 671 1267) at reasonable rates. Some have their own bathrooms and kitchens.

*before the number:*

*00 3531*

### ASTON HOTEL *sold out*

Tranquil hotel situated in the middle of Temple Bar that manages to convey a feeling of calm while all outside is hectic. Popular with groups. Top end of price range.

✚ d1 ✉ 7–9 Aston Quay ☎ 677 9300; fax 677 9007 🚌 Cross-city buses

### AVALON HOUSE

This purpose-built hostel offers single, double, and dormitory rooms, in neat, fresh surroundings. Facilities include a casual café and use of internet.

✚ b/c5 ✉ 55 Aungier Street ☎ 475 0001; fax 475 0303 🚌 Cross-city buses

### BARNACLES TEMPLE BAR HOUSE *sold out*

Hostel with communal TV room, self catering facilities, and breakfast room. All rooms come with own shower. Perfect for those into the buzz of Temple Bar.

✚ c2 ✉ 19 Temple Lane South ☎ 671 6277; fax 671 6591 🚉 Tara Street 🚌 Cross-city buses

### BEWLEY'S NEWLANDS CROSS *can*

Good amenities and spacious bedrooms, furnished to a high standard. Slightly outside the city so most suitable if you have a car.

✚ Off map to west ✉ Newland's Cross, Naas Road ☎ 464 0140; fax 464 0900 🚌 51, 51B, 69X

### HARDING HOTEL *sold out*

A superior find in the budget bracket, Hardings looks the part with clever interior design and is packed with atmosphere thanks to a really lively hotel bar.

✚ f8 ✉ Copper Alley, Fishamble Street ☎ 679 6500; fax 679 6504 🚌 Cross-city buses

### KINLAY HOUSE *sold out*

A good hostel with rooms to suit different budgets—from dormitory-style to en-suite twins. Continental breakfast included. Can be noisy at night.

✚ f/g8 ✉ 2–12 Lord Edward Street ☎ 679 6644; fax 679 7437 🚌 Cross-city buses

### MARIAN GUEST HOUSE *for*

In Georgian Dublin, 5 to 10 minutes' walk from the city centre and principal attractions. Family run, offering a warm welcome and tastefully decorated rooms with tea- and coffee-making facilities.

✚ J4 ✉ 21 Upper Gardiner Street ☎ 874 4129 🚉 Connolly 🚌 41A

### ORMOND QUAY HOTEL *120€*

Overlooking the River Liffey and offering a friendly and welcoming atmosphere. Comfortable rooms.

✚ b1 ✉ 7–11 Upper Ormond Quay ☎ 872 1811; fax 872 1362 🚉 Tara Street 🚌 Cross-city buses

### O'SHEAS

Warm and friendly hotel close to the shopping districts and visitor attractions. Attractive rooms, bar, lounge, and restaurant.

✚ L7 ✉ 19 Talbot Street ☎ 836 5670; fax 836 5214 🚉 Connolly 🚌 Cross-city buses

*O'Sheas Merchant:*
*679-3797*

# **DUBLIN**
# travel facts

## ESSENTIAL FACTS

### Customs regulations

- The limits for non-EU visitors are 200 cigarettes or 50 cigars, or 250g of tobacco; 1 litre of spirits (over 22 percent) or 2 litres of fortified wine, 2 litres of still wine; 50g of perfume. Travellers under 18 are not entitled to the tobacco and alcohol allowances. The guidelines for EU residents (for personal use) are 800 cigarettes, 200 cigars, 1kg tobacco; 10 litres of spirits (over 22 percent), 20 litres of aperitifs, 90 litres of wine, of which 60 can be sparkling wine, 110 litres of beer.

### Electricity

- 220V AC. Most hotels have 110V shaver outlets.
- Plugs are three square pins.

### Etiquette

- Dubliners are very friendly, so do not be unduly perturbed if strangers strike up conversation. Trust your instincts.
- Do not expect Dubliners to be very punctual. If you are invited to someone's home for dinner, aim to arrive about ten minutes after the agreed time.
- Groups of friends and acquaintances usually buy drinks in rounds and if you join them, you will be expected to participate.

### Gay and lesbian travellers

- *Gay Community News*, a free monthly newspaper, is available from clubs, bars, and bookshops.
- Gay and lesbian events in Dublin include the Alternative Miss Ireland (March), Pride (late June), and the Lesbian and Gay Film Festival (late July).
- For information and advice,

contact: Gay Switchboard Dublin ☎ 872 1055 🕐 Sun–Fri 8–10PM; Sat 3:30–6PM; Outhouse Gay Community and Resource Centre ✉ 105 Capel Street ☎ 873 4932

### Lone and women travellers

- Dublin is relatively safe but it's smart to be cautious.
- After dark, sit downstairs on buses or in a busy car on trains.
- Take a taxi rather than a late-night bus out to the suburbs.
- Keep to well-lit main streets. You may prefer to avoid Temple Bar at pub/club closing time. Not necessarily dangerous but mobs exiting to the streets may be intimidating.
- Do not stroll around Fitzwilliam and Merrion squares, or adjoining streets, late at night. They are prime prostitution areas.

### Money matters

- Banks offer better exchange rates than shops, hotels, and bureaux de change.
- The bank at Dublin airport has longer opening hours but charges above-average commission.
- Credit cards can be used in most hotels, shops, and restaurants and to withdraw cash from ATMs.
- Most large shops, hotels, and restaurants accept travellers' cheques accompanied by some form of identification.

### National holidays

- 1 January, 17 March, Good Friday, Easter Monday, first Monday in May, Whit Monday (first Mon in May/early June), first Monday in August, All Souls' Day (last Mon in October/1 November), 25 and 26 December.
- All pubs and most businesses close on Good Friday. Some shops stay open.

## Opening hours

- Museums and sights: open seven days a week, with shorter hours on Sunday. Call for details.
- Shops: six days a week, some seven days. Late-night shopping on Thursday. Supermarkets are open longer hours Wed–Fri. Large suburban shopping centres now also stay open Sunday 12–6.
- Banks: Mon–Fri 10–4; Thu 10–5.

## Places of worship

- Although Ireland is predominantly Catholic, most religious groups have places of worship in Dublin.
- Buddhism: Buddhist Centre ✉ 56 Inchicore Road ☎ 453 7427
- Church of Ireland: Christ Church Cathedral ✉ Christchurch Place ☎ 677 8099; St. Patrick's Cathedral ✉ Patrick's Close ☎ 475 4817; St. Ann's Church ✉ Dawson Street ☎ 676 7727
- Methodist: ✉ 9c Lower Abbey Street ☎ 874 2123
- Muslim: Mosque ✉ 163 South Circular Road ☎ 453 3242
- Roman Catholic: St. Mary's Pro-Cathedral ✉ Marlborough Street ☎ 874 5441; University Church ✉ 87a St. Stephen's Green ☎ 478 0616; St. Teresa's Church ✉ Clarendon Street, off Grafton Street

## Restrooms

- Dublin is not renowned for the quality or quantity of its public conveniences. Most people go to a pub or large store.
- Signs may be in Irish: *mná*: women, *fir*: men.

## Student travellers

- Dublin is very student-friendly.
- An International Student Identity Card secures discounts in many cinemas, theatres, shops, restaurants, and attractions.
- Discounts may be available on travel cards for the bus and DART.

## Tipping

- Tips are not expected in cinemas, petrol stations, or in pubs, unless there is table service.
- 10 per cent is customary for hairdressers and taxi drivers; porters, doormen, and clockroom attendants €2.
- (► 64 for restaurant tipping.)

## Tourist information

- ✉ Dublin Airport; ✉ Suffolk Street; ✉ Dun Laoghaire Harbour; ✉ Baggot Street Bridge; ✉ The Square, Tallaght Town Centre For visitor information: ☎ 1850 230 330 (within Ireland) or 00 353 669 792 083 (from USA); website: www.visitdublin.com

## GETTING ABOUT

### Buses

- Dublin Bus (Bus Átha Cliath) operates Mon–Sat 7AM–11.30PM, Sun 10AM–11.30PM ☎ 873 4222
- The Nitelink service operates Thu to Sat to the suburbs. Buses leave on the hour from College Street, D'Olier Street, and Westmoreland Street from midnight until 3.30AM.
- Bus Éireann operates a nationwide coach service that runs from other cities in Ireland ☎ 836 6111.

### Passes or tickets

- Irish Rail and Dublin Bus sell a range of combined travel passes—single, family, one-day, four-day, weekly (photograph needed). They are not valid for *Nitelink*, *Airlink*, ferry services, or tours.
- You can buy all travel passes from Dublin Bus ✉ 55 Upper O'Connell Street. Selected newsstands sell a limited number of passes.

## Taxis

- Useful numbers: All Sevens Taxi
  ☎ 677 7777; Metro ☎ 668 3333;
  National Radio Cabs ☎ 677 2222;
  VIP Radio Taxis ☎ 478 3333.
  See local telephone books for
  others.

## MEDIA & COMMUNICATIONS

### Posting a letter

- Stamps are sold at post offices,
  some newsstands, hotels, and
  shops. Books of stamps are available from coin-operated machines
  outside some post offices.
- Postboxes are green.
- The GPO in O'Connell Street
  is open Mon–Sat 8–8, Sun 10–6.30.
  Other post offices are generally
  open Mon–Fri 9–5.30 and certain
  city-centre branches open on
  Saturdays. Some suburban offices
  close for an hour at lunchtime.

### Newspapers and magazines

- The daily broadsheets, the *Irish
  Times* and the *Irish Independent*, are
  printed in Dublin. The *Evening
  Herald* is on sale Mon–Fri at mid-
  day. The major UK tabloids also
  produce separate Irish editions.
- International magazines and newspapers are sold in: Easons ✉ 40–2
  Lower O'Connell Street and Tuthills
  ✉ Royal Hibernian Way
- For events and entertainment listings, check out *In Dublin* and the
  free *Event Guide*.
- *Hot Press* is Ireland's music
  magazine, *dSide* is read by fashion-
  conscious club kids, and *Image* is
  Ireland's best-selling women's
  magazine.

### Telephones

- Public telephones use coins or
  phone cards (sold in post offices
  and news dealers).

- Operator ☎ 10; inland directory
  enquiries ☎ 11850; UK and
  overseas directory enquiries
  ☎ 11860
- Avoid calling from hotels where
  charges are high. Look for public
  phones on streets, in pubs, and
  shopping centres.
- The following may be used in
  front of local telephone numbers:
  freefone ☎ 1800.
- When calling from the UK dial 00
  353. The code for Dublin is 01
  (omit the zero when calling from
  abroad).
- To call the UK from Dublin , dial
  00 44.
- When calling from the US dial 011
  353. The code for Dublin is 01
  (omit the zero when calling from
  abroad).
- To call the US from Dublin, dial
  00 1.

### Television and radio

- Radio Telefís Éireann (RTÉ) is
  the state broadcasting authority. It
  has three radio stations and three
  television channels.
- Its television channels are: RTÉ 1
  (mainstream), N2 (aimed at
  younger, trendier viewers), and
  the Irish-speaking *Telefís Na Gaeilge
  (TnaG)*.
- Independent radio stations: Today
  FM (100–102 MHz), FM104, and
  98FM.

## EMERGENCIES

### Emergency phone numbers

- Police (garda), fire, and ambulance
  ☎ 999 (free of charge).

### Embassies

- Australia ✉ Fitzwilton House, Wilton Place,
  Dublin 2 ☎ 676 1517
- Belgium ✉ Shrewsbury Road, Dublin 4
  ☎ 269 2082

- Canada ✉ St. Stephen's Green, Dublin 2
  ☎ 478 4100
- Denmark ✉ 121 St. Stephen's Green,
  Dublin 2 ☎ 475 6404
- Finland ✉ Russell House, Stokes Place,
  Dublin 2 ☎ 478 1344
- France ✉ 36 Ailesbury Road, Dublin 4
  ☎ 260 1666
- Germany ✉ 31 Trimleston Avenue,
  Booterstown, County Dublin ☎ 269 3011
- Greece ✉ 1 Upper Pembroke Street,
  Dublin 2 ☎ 676 7254
- Italy ✉ 63 Northumberland Road, Dublin 4
  ☎ 660 1744
- Japan ✉ Nutley Building, Merrion Court,
  Dublin 4 ☎ 269 4244
- Netherlands ✉ 106 Merrion Road,
  Dublin 4 ☎ 269 3444
- Russia ✉ 184–186 Orwell Road, Dublin 14
  ☎ 492 3525
- Spain ✉ 17a Merlyn Park, Sandymount,
  Dublin 4 ☎ 269 1640
- United Kingdom ✉ 39 Merrion Road,
  Dublin 4 ☎ 205 3700
- US ✉ 42 Elgin Road, Ballsbridge, Dublin 4
  ☎ 668 8777

### Lost property

- Report loss or theft of a passport to
  the police immediately. Your
  embassy or consulate can provide
  further assistance.
- Airport ☎ 814 4480; ferryport ☎ 855
  2296 or ☎ 661 0511; train ☎ 836 3333;
  bus, Dublin Bus ☎ 703 1321, Bus
  Éireann ☎ 836 6111

### Medicines and medical treatment

- Ambulance ☎ 999 or 112.
- Hospital with 24-hour emergency
  service: St. Vincent's ✉ Elm Park,
  Dublin 4 ☎ 269 4533
- Daytime dental facilities: Dental
  Hospital ✉ 20 Lincoln Place ☎ 662 0766
  For dental referrals: Irish Dental
  Association ✉ Richview, Clonskeagh Road,
  Dublin 4 ☎ 283 0499 .
- Minor ailments can usually be
  treated at pharmacies but only a

limited range of medication can be
dispensed without a prescription.
- Pharmacies open until 10PM:
  O'Connell Pharmacy ✉ 55 Lower
  O'Connell Street, Dublin 1 ☎ 873 0427;
  Donnybrook Pharmacy ✉ 8 The Mall,
  Donnybrook, Dublin 4 ☎ 269 5236

### Sensible precautions

- Pickpockets and bag snatching are
  prevalent.
- Keep valuables out of sight.
- Watch handbags and wallets in
  restaurants, hotels, cafés, shops,
  and cinemas.
- Make a separate note of all
  passport, ticket, travellers'
  cheques, and credit card numbers.
- Avoid Phoenix Park after dark.

## LANGUAGE

Although the Irish language is still
alive and studied by all school
children, English is the spoken
language in Dublin. Irish is rarely
spoken, but the language is enjoying
a revival and is fashionable among a
younger set proud of their cultural
traditions. You will come across Irish
on signposts, buses, trains, and official documents and the news (*an
nuacht*) is broadcast *as gaeilge* on television and radio. *Telefís Na Gaeilge* is a
dedicated Irish language channel
with English subtitles.
Some Irish words to look out for:

| | |
|---|---|
| An Lar | City Centre |
| Baile Átha Cliath | Dublin |
| Céilí | Dance |
| Craic | Fun; laughter; good time |
| Leitris | Lavatory |
| Mná: | Ladies |
| Fir: | Gents |
| Dia dhuit | Hello |
| Slán | Goodbye |
| Sláinte | Cheers |

93

# Index

# CityPack Dublin

## ABOUT THE AUTHORS

Dr Peter Harbison, Honorary Editor of the Royal Irish Academy, is a former editor of *Ireland of the Welcomes* magazine. He is the author of numerous books on Irish archaeology, art and architecture. *Ancient Ireland* (1996), a book he co-edited with photographer Jacqueline O'Brien, has appeared in English and German. Melanie Morris is the publisher and editor of *dSide*, Ireland's leading style magazine.

**CONTRIBUTIONS TO "LIVING DUBLIN"**   Hilary Weston and Jackie Staddon
**COVER DESIGN**   Tigist Getachew, Fabrizio La Rocca
**EDITION REVISERS**   Bookmark Associates

A CIP catalogue record for this book is available from the British Library.

**ISBN 0 7495 3569 5**

The contents of this publication are believed correct at the time of printing. Nevertheless, the publishers cannot be held responsible for any errors or omissions or for changes in the details given in this guide or for the consequences of any reliance on the information provided by the same. This does not affect your statutory rights. Assessments of attractions, hotels, restaurants and so forth are based upon the author's own personal experience and, therefore, descriptions given in this guide necessarily contain an element of subjective opinion which may not reflect the publishers' opinion or dictate a reader's own experiences on another occasion. We have tried to ensure accuracy in this guide, but things do change and we would be grateful if readers would advise us of any inaccuracies they may encounter.

Published by AA Publishing (a trading name of Automobile Association Developments Limited, whose registered office is Millstream, Maidenhead Road, Windsor, Berkshire, SL4 5GD. Registered number 1878835).

© **AUTOMOBILE ASSOCIATION DEVELOPMENTS LIMITED 1999, 2001, 2003**
First published 1999. Revised second edition 2001. Revised third edition 2003.

Colour separation by Daylight Colour Art Pte Ltd, Singapore
Printed and bound by Dai Nippon Printing Co (Hong Kong) Ltd.

## ACKNOWLEDGEMENTS

The Automobile Association would like to thank the following photographers, libraries and associations for their assistance in the preparation of this book:
THE BOARD OF TRINITY COLLEGE, DUBLIN 44t; BORD FAILTE 27t, 43t; DUBLINIA, NORTON ASSOCIATES 31t, 31b; DUCHAS, THE HERITAGE SERVICE 50b; HULTON ARCHIVE 16c, 17; MARY EVANS PICTURE LIBRARY 16l, 16/17; NATIONAL GALLERY OF IRELAND 48; NATIONAL MUSEUM OF IRELAND 28b, 46b; NUMBER TWENTY NINE MUSEUM 49t; REX FEATURES LTD 62; STOCKBYTE 5. By kind permission of Guinness Ltd 27t, 27b, 63b. The remaining pictures are held in the Association's own library (AA PHOTO LIBRARY) were taken by STEVE DAY with the exception of 21c, 51b LIAM BLAKE; cover: blurred image CHRIS COE; 39b, 63t T KING; 10l, 10r, 11l, 15c, 20c, 22tc, 22tr SIMON McBRIDE; cover: Façade College Green 7t, 15tc, 21t, 25b, 32t, 35b, 40t, 40b, 45b, 47, 47b, 56, 58, 59, 89t MICHAEL SHORT; 8lb, 30, 35t, 36b, 37t, 37b, 41b, 51t, 52, 53, 59b SLIDE FILE; cover: James Joyce statue, Irish Stout sign 10c, 25t WYN VOYSEY; cover: Custom House, Front Door, Christchurch Cathedral, St Audeons church, back cover 15b, 19c, 26t, 26b, 27b, 28t, 32c, 33t, 33c, 34b, 38, 39t, 42t, 42b, 43b, 44t, 45t, 46t, 49b, 50t, 54, 55, 57, 60, 61, 63b, 89b STEPHEN WHITEHORNE

A01084
Maps reproduced by permission of the Director of Ordnance Survey Ireland
© Ordnance Survey Ireland and Government of Ireland (Permit No. 7469).
Transport map © TCS, Aldershot, England

## TITLES IN THE CITYPACK SERIES